SPECTRUM®

Spelling

Grade 2

Spectrum®
an imprint of Carson Dellosa Education
Greensboro, NC

Spectrum®
An imprint of Carson Dellosa Education
P.O. Box 35665
Greensboro, NC 27425 USA

ISBN 978-1-4838-1175-8

03-081217784

Table of Contents Grade 2

Table of Contents, continued

The short **a** sound: b**a**g, d**a**d
The short **e** sound: b**e**d, h**e**n
The short **i** sound: p**i**g, **i**s
The short **o** sound: p**o**t, b**o**x
The /ô/ sound: d**o**g, l**o**st
The short **u** sound: s**u**n, t**u**b

The long **a** sound: l**a**k**e**, st**ay**, w**ai**t
The long **e** sound: m**e**, f**ee**t, **ea**t
The long **i** sound: l**i**k**e**, m**y**, n**i**ght
The long **o** sound: h**o**m**e**, n**o**, sl**ow**, c**oa**t

The /ü/ sound: r**oo**m, r**u**d**e**
The /ù/ sound: p**u**t, l**oo**k
The /ou/ sound: **ou**t, n**ow**

The /är/ sound: j**ar**, p**ar**k
The /ôr/ sound: f**or**t, m**or**e
The /ûr/ sound: g**ir**l, f**ir**st

The /k/ sound: **c**at, **k**ite, bla**ck**
The /s/ sound: ni**c**e, hou**s**e
The /z/ sound: **z**oo, u**s**e, no**s**e

The /th/ sound: **th**ing, wi**th**
The /wh/ sound: **wh**y, **wh**ite
The /sh/ sound: **sh**ip, di**sh**
The /ch/ sound: **ch**ild, tea**ch**

Lesson 1 Words with the Short a Sound

Say each word. Listen to the short **a** sound. Write the word.

Spelling Tip	The short **a** sound is often spelled **a**. The sign for short **a** is /a/.

Spelling Words

has   _____

man   _____

ham   _____

hat   _____

pan   _____

mad   _____

as   _____

jam   _____

bad   _____

pat   _____

Lesson 1 Words with the Short **a** Sound

Words in Context

Write the missing spelling words to finish the rhyme.

My Dad and His Cat

My dad is a _____.

He _____ a pet cat.

The cat's name is Nan.

She likes to chase rats.

My dad's really _____.

Nan chewed up his _____.

That cat is so _____,

I won't give her a _____.

_____ soon as he can,

Dad will make bread and _____.

He will get out a _____,

And then cook some _____.

> ### Challenge
> Circle the other words in the rhyme with the short **a** sound.

Lesson 1 Words with the Short **a** Sound

Fun with Words

Write the spelling word that goes with each word.

1. eggs   _____   **4.** bread   _____

2. pot   _____   **5.** woman _____

3. coat   _____   **6.** pet   _____

Write the spelling word that means the opposite of each word.

1. good   _____

2. glad   _____

Words Across the Curriculum

Say each social studies word. Then, write each word.

1. map   _____   **3.** cash   _____

2. path   _____   **4.** chat   _____

Write each social studies word where it belongs.

1. We will walk on the garden _____.

2. Coins and dollars are _____.

3. A _____ shows the state you live in.

4. Do you like to _____ with friends?

Lesson 1 Words with the Short **a** Sound

Words in Writing

Do you have to do chores at home? Write
a list of chores that must be done at home.
Use at least three words from the box.

has	ham	pan	as	bad	map	cash
man	hat	mad	jam	pat	path	chat

_____

_____

_____

_____

Misspelled Words

Read the student's list of things to do after school. Circle the five
misspelled words. Then, write the words correctly on the lines.

1. Put away my coat and het.   _____

2. Make a snack of bread and jem.   _____

3. Clean every pot and pen in the sink. _____

4. Pate my cat as soon as I find her.   _____

5. Walk my dog on the peth in the park. _____

Lesson 2 Words with the Short i Sound

Say each word. Listen to the short **i** sound. Write the word.

Spelling Tip	The short **i** sound is often spelled **i**. The sign for short **i** is /i/.

Spelling Words

pin   _____

sit   _____

fix   _____

will   _____

zip   _____

dish   _____

his   _____

rip   _____

hid   _____

wish   _____

Lesson 2 Words with the Short i Sound

Words in Context

Write the missing spelling words.

A Bad Day

Challenge

Circle the other words in the paragraph with the short **i** sound.

Today has been a bad day. I _____ be glad when

it's over. As I made lunch, I broke a _____. Just as I was

about to _____ down and eat, I stepped on a tack.

After lunch, I tried to give my cat a bath. He ran outside and

_____ from me because he doesn't like to get

_____ fur wet. As I started to _____ up

my coat, I saw a big _____ in it. I had to

_____ it with a _____. I

_____ this day would end soon!

Word Building

Add **p**, **g**, **t**, or **ll** to make new words.

1. si _____

2. wi _____

3. hi _____

4. ti _____

5. di _____

6. fi _____

7. ji _____

8. bi _____

Lesson 2 Words with the Short i Sound

Fun with Words

Unscramble the letters to make the spelling words.

1. dhi   _____   **6.** ist   _____

2. pri   _____   **7.** lilw   _____

3. xif   _____   **8.** pzi   _____

4. nip   _____   **9.** sdhi   _____

5. swih   _____   **10.** shi   _____

Words Across the Curriculum

Say each science word. Then, write each word.

1. fish   _____   **3.** mix   _____

2. milk   _____   **4.** pit   _____

Write each science word next to its definition.

1. to blend together   _____

2. a drink that comes from cows   _____

3. a water animal with fins   _____

4. the seed in a plum   _____

Lesson 2 Words with the Short i Sound

Words in Writing

Make up a silly rhyme. Use at least three words from the box.

pin	fix	zip	his	hid	fish	milk
sit	will	dish	rip	wish	mix	pit

_____

_____

_____

_____

_____

Misspelled Words

Read the rhyme. Circle the four misspelled words. Then, write the words correctly on the lines.

1. Tim had a wiss.   _____

2. He wished for a fesh.   _____

3. When he looked at hes dishe. _____

4. One appeared with a swish!   _____

Lesson 3 Words with the Short o and /ô/ Sounds

Say each word. Listen to the middle sound. Write the word.

Spelling Tip	The short **o** sound and the /ô/ sound are often spelled **o**. The sign for short **o** is /o/. /o/ sound: h**o**p /ô/ sound: d**o**g

Spelling Words

hop   _____

lot   _____

jog   _____

got   _____

dog   _____

spot   _____

off   _____

lost   _____

soft   _____

long   _____

Lesson 3 Words with the Short **o** and /ô/ Sounds

Words in Context
Write the missing spelling words.

My Lost Dog

When I _____ up today, I could not find my

_____ Moll. She was _____! I took a

_____ around the block to look for her. After a

_____ time, I saw Moll. Her collar was coming

_____ her neck. She had a _____ of mud all

over her legs. One foot was hurt. Moll had to _____ on

three legs. I patted her _____ fur and

rubbed the hurt _____ on her foot.

Word Building
Add **s** to tell what a girl is doing. Then, write the word.

1. I jog. She jog_____.   _____

2. I hop. She hop_____.   _____

3. I mop. She mop_____.   _____

4. I chop. She chop_____.   _____

5. I shop. She shop_____.   _____

Lesson 3 Words with the Short **o** and /ô/ Sounds

Fun with Words

Write the spelling word that means the opposite.

1. on _____

3. short _____

2. hard _____

4. found _____

Write the spelling word or words that rhyme with each word.

1. top _____

2. hog _____ _____

3. not _____ _____

_____

Words Across the Curriculum

Say each science word. Then, write each word.

1. fox _____

3. fog _____

2. hot _____

4. robin _____

Write the science word that belongs with each pair of words.

1. rain, dew _____

2. bluebird, crow _____

3. warm, burning, _____

4. dog, wolf _____

Lesson 3 Words with the Short **o** and /ô/ Sounds

Words in Writing

Have you ever lost a pet? Make a poster that tells about a lost pet. Use at least three words from the box.

_____

_____

_____

_____

_____

hop	jog	dog	off	soft	fox	fog
lot	got	spot	lost	long	hot	robin

Dictionary Practice

Words in the dictionary are in ABC order. Write the word from the box that comes between each pair of words.

1. pan   _____   soft

2. hug   _____   lap

3. fox   _____   hat

4. long   _____   lot

5. mop   _____   pit

Lesson 4 Words with the Final /k/ Sound

Say each word. Listen to the ending sound. Write the word.

Spelling Tip	The /k/ sound at the end of a word is often spelled **ck**.

Spelling Words

sack   _____

pack   _____

rock   _____

back   _____

chick   _____

pick   _____

stick   _____

flock   _____

snack   _____

peck   _____

Lesson 4 Words with the Final /k/ Sound

Words in Context

Write the missing spelling words.

At the Farm

Challenge

Circle the other words in the journal entry with the /k/ sound.

Today, I went to _____ apples from

trees on a farm. I had to _____ them

all in a big _____. Then, I sat on a

_____. I ate a stack of crackers for

a _____. A _____ of black birds landed

near me. One little bird was only a _____. It turned its

neck and saw a brown _____ on the ground. The baby

bird began to _____ at it with its beak. Then, it ran

_____ to its mother.

Word Building

Add **s** to each word to make words that tell about more than one.

1. one pack, two _____

2. one chick, two _____

3. one rock, two _____

4. one flock, two _____

5. one snack, two _____

Lesson 4 Words with the Final /k/ Sound

Fun with Words

Each word below has at least one spelling word in it. Circle each spelling word that you find.

1. chicken

2. picking

3. packer

4. snacking

5. sticky

6. backpack

7. rocky

8. flocked

9. rocker

10. pecking

Words Across the Curriculum

Say each social studies word. Then, write each word.

1. lock _____

2. shack _____

3. clock _____

4. tack _____

Write each social studies word next to the pair of words it belongs with.

1. time, watch _____

2. pin, nail _____

3. shut, bolt _____

4. home, hut _____

Lesson 4 Words with the Final /k/ Sound

Words in Writing

Write about some things you might see and do on a farm. Use at least three words from the box.

sack	rock	chick	stick	snack	lock	clock
pack	back	pick	flock	peck	shack	tack

_____

_____

_____

_____

_____

Misspelled Words

Read the student's list of jobs she does on her farm. Circle the five misspelled words. Then, write the words correctly on the lines.

1. Feed the fleck of ducks

 and the chiks.   _____

2. Pick up the stecks and

 rocs in the yard.   _____

                                   _____

3. Pak the eggs in a box.   _____

Lesson 5 Words with **nd** and **st**

Say each word. Listen to the **nd** and **st** sounds. Write the word.

Spelling Tip	The **nd** and **st** sounds are spelled **nd** and **st**.

Spelling Words

fast _____

list _____

band _____

past _____

fist _____

pond _____

last _____

stand _____

cast _____

stack _____

Lesson 5 Words with **nd** and **st**

Words in Context

Write the missing spelling words.

A Day at the Fair

Challenge

Circle the other words in the journal entry with **nd** or **st**.

_____ week, I went to the fair. I

heard a _____ play music. Then, I went

to a food _____. It had a sign with a

_____ of good things to eat. I decided to

have a _____ of pancakes and some

milk. I couldn't eat very _____ because I

had a _____ on my broken hand. I couldn't make a

_____ to hold my fork. After I ate, I just watched some

ducks as I walked _____ the _____.

Word Building

Add **nd** or **st** to make new words. Then, write the words.

1. ki_____   _____

2. _____ir   _____

3. _____amp   _____

4. se_____   _____

Lesson 5 Words with **nd** and **st**

Fun with Words

Use the clues to solve the puzzle with spelling words.

Down

1. opposite of slow

3. a small lake

4. a pile

6. a note of things to do

Across

2. opposite of sit

3. by

5. a wrap for a broken bone

6. opposite of first

Words Across the Curriculum

Say each science word. Then, write each word.

1. sand _____ **3.** land _____

2. wind _____ **4.** mist _____

Write the missing science words.

1. Fog is a _____ of tiny water drops.

2. Earth has oceans and _____.

3. _____ is moving air.

4. Beaches have _____ instead of dirt.

Lesson 5 Words with **nd** and **st**

Words in Writing

Why do people like to go camping?
Write an ad that tells why a campsite is
fun. Use at least three words from the box.

| fast | band | fist | last | cast | sand | land |
| list | past | pond | stand | stack | wind | mist |

_____

_____

_____

_____

Misspelled Words

Read the student's ad for a campsite. Circle the six misspelled words.
Then, write the words on the lines below.

This is your last chance to get a good campsite! We have a pon
where you can go fishing. You can fish from a boat or from the lande. If
the wid and miste make you cold, you can make a campfire. There is a
stak of wood that you can use. Call us soon. These campsites will go fasst!

_____   _____   _____

_____   _____   _____

Review Lessons 1–5

Write the five spelling words that rhyme with **tack**.

1. _____

2. _____

3. _____

4. _____

5. _____

Write the spelling word that means the opposite of each word.

1. first _____

2. on _____

3. happy _____

4. break _____

5. sit _____

6. found _____

7. slow _____

8. won't _____

9. good _____

10. short _____

Review Lessons 1–5

Write the spelling word that belongs with each pair of words.

1. want, hope _____

2. walk, run _____

3. mine, hers _____

4. plate, bowl _____

5. stone, pebble _____

6. tear, cut _____

7. pot, kettle _____

8. boy, woman _____

Write the spelling word that fits in each sentence.

1. A _____ of birds landed near me.

2. The cat has _____, fluffy fur.

3. I will _____ flowers for my mom.

4. The fish swam in the _____.

5. My dad made a _____ of jobs for me to do.

6. I like _____ on my toast.

7. My dog has a white _____ on his face.

8. I will _____ up my coat.

Lesson 6 Words with the Short **u** Sound

Say each word. Listen for the short **u** sound. Write the word.

Spelling Tip	The short **u** sound is often spelled **u**. The sign for short **u** is /u/.

Spelling Words

us   _____

rug   _____

luck   _____

tug   _____

must   _____

hunt   _____

bug   _____

duck   _____

stuck   _____

lunch   _____

Lesson 6 Words with the Short u Sound

Words in Context

Write the missing spelling words.

Good Luck for a Bug

My friend Russ and I went to the park. We stopped near the pond to eat our _____. We spread a blanket like a

_____ on the grass. We had to _____ on the ends to smooth out the blanket. As we ate, we saw a

_____ swim toward _____. Then, it started to _____ for something to eat. The duck saw a small water _____. The duck rushed toward the bug, but it got _____ in some mud. The bug swam away. It _____ have had really good _____!

Word Building

Add **s** to each word to make words that tell about more than one.

1. one bug, two _____

2. one duck, two _____

3. one hut, two _____

4. one tub, two _____

5. one hug, two _____

Lesson 6 Words with the Short **u** Sound

Fun with Words

Change the vowel in each word to make a spelling word.

1. mist   _____

2. is   _____

3. rag   _____

4. hint   _____

5. lick   _____

6. tag   _____

7. big   _____

8. stack   _____

Words Across the Curriculum

Say each math word. Then, write each word.

1. sum   _____   **3.** number _____

2. plus   _____   **4.** subtract_____

Write the missing math words.

When you add one _____ to another, you find the

_____. You use a _____ sign to show that

you are adding. You use a minus sign when you _____.

Lesson 6 Words with the Short **u** Sound

Words in Writing

Write about a good day you had. Use
at least three words from the box.

us	luck	must	bug	stuck	sum	number
rug	tug	hunt	duck	lunch	plus	subtract

_____

_____

_____

_____

Dictionary Practice

Write each word from the box in ABC order.

BCDEFGHI   **JKLMNOPQ**   **RSTUVWXYZ**

_____   _____   _____

_____   _____   _____

_____   _____   _____

_____   _____

_____

Lesson 7 Words with the Short e Sound

Say each word. Listen for the short **e** sound. Write the word.

Spelling Tip	The short **e** sound is often spelled **e**. The sign for short **e** is /e/.

Spelling Words

pen   _____

met   _____

rest   _____

send   _____

yet   _____

tell   _____

them   _____

went   _____

best   _____

mess   _____

Lesson 7 Words with the Short **e** Sound

Words in Context

Write the missing spelling words.

At the Pet Shop

Challenge

Circle the other words in the letter with the short **e** sound.

Dear Meg,

I have to _____ you

about my trip to the pet shop. I

_____ there yesterday and

_____ my friend Rick. We

saw some pups playing in a _____. After a while, they

sat down to _____. They were so cute that I wanted to

take all of _____ home. I called Mom to see if I could

get one pup. I promised not to let it make a _____ in

the house. I told Mom it would be the _____ birthday

present she could get me. She said yes! I haven't named my new

pup _____. _____ me a letter soon!

Love,
Ben

Lesson 7 Words with the Short e Sound

Fun with Words

Unscramble the letters to make spelling words.

1. netw _____
2. lelt _____
3. tye _____
4. sems _____

5. steb _____
6. emt _____
7. tres _____
8. ndes _____

Words Across the Curriculum

Say each math word. Then, write each word.

1. set _____
2. less _____

3. lend _____
4. spend _____

Write the missing math words.

1. A bank can _____ money to people.

2. The number six is _____ than the number eight.

3. You can _____ money or save it.

4. A _____ is a group of things.

Lesson 7 Words with the Short e Sound

Words in Writing

Write a letter to a friend. Use at
least three words from the box.

pen	rest	yet	them	best	set	lend
met	send	tell	went	mess	less	spend

_____

_____

_____

Misspelled Words

Read the student's letter. Circle the five misspelled words. Then, write
the words correctly.

Dear Jen,

   I've been waiting for you to sen me a postcard, but I haven't
gotten one yet. I bet this will be the besst summer you've ever had! I
mett a lot of friends when I wente to the beach. Write soon to till me
all about your trip.

Your friend,
Beth

_____   _____   _____

_____   _____

Lesson 8 Words with **dr**, **gr**, and **tr**

Say each word. Listen to the beginning sound. Write the word.

Spelling Tip	The /dr/, /gr/, and /tr/ sounds are spelled **dr**, **gr**, and **tr**.

Spelling Words

drop   _____

trap   _____

dry   _____

grin   _____

drum   _____

trip   _____

grip   _____

trick   _____

try   _____

dress   _____

Lesson 8 Words with **dr**, **gr**, and **tr**

Words in Context

Write the missing spelling words.

Challenge

Circle the other words in the story with **dr**, **gr**, or **tr**.

A Tricky Friend

I met a friend named Greg on my _____ to camp.

Greg would always _____ to play a

_____ on me. One time, I was playing my

_____. I did not see Greg _____ a spider

and take it from its web. Greg put the spider on my

_____. The spider really startled me! It made me lose

my _____ on my drumsticks and _____

them. My mouth was so _____

I couldn't scream. Greg just looked at me with

a great big _____ on his face.

Word Building

Add **dr**, **gr**, or **tr** to make new words. Then, write the new words.

1. _____ip _____
2. _____uck _____
3. _____eat _____
4. _____im _____
5. _____ive _____
6. _____ack _____

Lesson 8 Words with dr, gr, and tr

Fun with Words

Add and subtract the letters to make spelling words.

1. chin – ch + gr = _____

2. mess – m + dr = _____

3. ripe + t – e = _____

4. plum – pl + dr = _____

5. chick – ch + tr = _____

6. rope + d – e = _____

7. map – m + tr = _____

8. chip – ch + gr = _____

Words Across the Curriculum

Say each science word. Then, write each word.

1. tree _____   **3.** grass _____

2. grow _____   **4.** gram _____

Write the missing science words.

A _____ is a tall plant with a trunk and leaves. One

big leaf might weigh about one _____.

_____ is a short plant that can _____

very fast.

Lesson 8 Words with **dr**, **gr**, and **tr**

Words in Writing

Write a funny story about a trick that a pet can do. Use at least three words from the box.

_____

_____

_____

_____

drop	dry	drum	grip	try	tree	grass
trap	grin	trip	trick	dress	grow	gram

Dictionary Practice

A dictionary has symbols that tell how to say words. Write the word or words from the box that have the sound of each short-vowel symbol.

/a/ _____ _____ _____

/e/ _____

/i/ _____ _____ _____

_____

/o/ _____

/u/ _____

Lesson 9 Words with **bl**, **gl**, and **pl**

Say each word. Listen to the beginning sound. Write the word.

Spelling Tip	The **bl**, **gl**, and **pl** sounds are spelled the way they sound.

Spelling Words

plum _____

glass _____

bloom _____

glow _____

glad _____

plan _____

block _____

plot _____

glove _____

plant _____

Lesson 9 Words with bl, gl, and pl

Words in Context
Write the missing spelling words.

An Indoor Garden

I drew a _____ for an indoor garden. It will be in

a room with plenty of windows made of _____. The

windows won't _____ the _____ of the

sun. First, I will _____ a _____ tree. I'll

wear a _____ on one hand when I place the tree in

the rich, black dirt. My garden will also have a _____

for flowers. Everyone will be _____

when they _____.

Word Building
Add **es** to make words that mean more than one. Then, write the new words.

1. one glass, two glass_____   _____

2. one dress, two dress_____   _____

3. one fox, two fox_____   _____

4. one class, two class_____   _____

5. one lunch, two lunch_____   _____

Lesson 9 Words with **bl**, **gl**, and **pl**

Fun with Words

Circle the hidden spelling words.

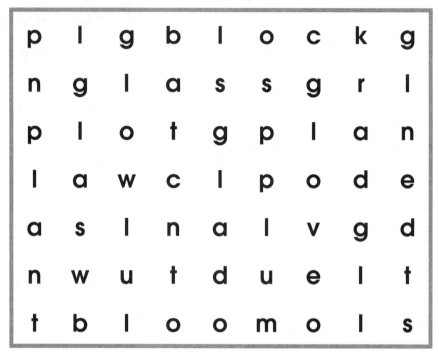

p	l	g	b	l	o	c	k	g
n	g	l	a	s	s	g	r	l
p	l	o	t	g	p	l	a	n
l	a	w	c	l	p	o	d	e
a	s	l	n	a	l	v	g	d
n	w	u	t	d	u	e	l	t
t	b	l	o	o	m	o	l	s

Words Across the Curriculum

Say each art word. Then, write each word.

1. blot _____   **3.** blank _____

2. blend _____

Write the art words where they belong.

You can create a colorful picture on a _____ sheet

of paper. You can _____ different colors of paint

together. You can use a cloth to _____ the paint dry.

Lesson 9 Words with **bl**, **gl**, and **pl**

Words in Writing

Write a description of an artwork you made.
Use at least three of the words from the box.

_____

_____

_____

_____

_____

plum	bloom	glad	block	glove	blot	blank
glass	glow	plan	plot	plant	blend	

Dictionary Practice

Some words have more than one meaning. A dictionary tells all the
meanings of words. Write the word from the box next to its two meanings.

1. the action in a story; a small piece of ground _____

2. a square piece of wood; to be in the way _____

3. a living thing that has leaves; to put in the ground _____

4. something to drink from; what a window is made of _____

Lesson 10 Words with **mp**, **ng**, and **sk**

Say each word. Listen to the ending sound. Write the word.

| Spelling Tip | The /mp/, /ng/, and /sk/ sounds are spelled **ng**, **mp**, and **sk**. |

Spelling Words

ask   _____

camp   _____

wing   _____

desk   _____

sting   _____

jump   _____

lamp   _____

bring   _____

dump   _____

ramp   _____

Lesson 10 Words with **mp**, **ng**, and **sk**

Words in Context

Write the missing spelling words.

Fun Away from Home

Challenge

Circle the other words in the story with **ng**, **mp**, or **sk**.

Dear Carlos,

I'm having a great time at _____! In the morning,

we run down a long _____ and _____

into the lake. Then, we each have to do a task. I have to

_____ the trash outside. Then, I _____ it

in a large bin. Once, there was a pesky bee with a black spot on one

_____ near the bin. I was afraid it might

_____ me, but it flew away. At night, we sing songs or

perform funny skits. I sit at the _____ in my room. I turn

on the _____ and read a book. You should

_____ your mom if you

can come to camp next year.

Your friend,
Mike

Lesson 10 Words with **mp**, **ng**, and **sk**

Fun with Words

Write the spelling word that fits each tongue-twister.

1. Can Carlos come to _____?

2. Don't _____ dirt down the drain.

3. Ron ran in the rain on the _____.

4. _____ Brad the broken brown branch.

5. Jack will just _____ over Jim's jeep.

6. Lily looked at the light leaving the _____.

7. _____ Ann to add all the apples.

8. One _____ of the wasp was white.

Words Across the Curriculum

Say each art word. Then, write each word.

1. song   _____   3. ring   _____

2. mask   _____   4. lump   _____

Write each art word next to the correct clue.

1. This could be a piece of clay.   _____

2. You can sing this.   _____

3. This hides your face.   _____

4. A bell makes this sound.   _____

Lesson 10 Words with mp, ng, and sk

Words in Writing

Write some questions that you would ask a camp worker about a camp you might like to visit. Use at least three words from the box.

ask	wing	sting	lamp	dump	song	ring
camp	desk	jump	bring	ramp	mask	lump

_____

_____

_____

_____

Misspelled Words

Read the student's questions. Circle the six misspelled words. Then, write the words correctly.

1. Are there any bugs that can stinge? _____

2. Should I breng _____

   my own lammp? _____

3. Do you have a desck that I can use? _____

4. Do we have to aks before we jemp _____

   in the lake? _____

Review Lessons 6–10

Write the spelling word that belongs with each pair of words.

1. hat, scarf, _____

2. guitar, trumpet, _____

3. apple, peach, _____

4. hop, skip, _____

5. smile, laugh, _____

6. shirt, pants, _____

Write the spelling word that rhymes with each pair of words.

1. bent, sent, _____

2. rust, just, _____

3. mad, sad, _____

4. lip, drip, _____

5. nest, pest, _____

6. blot, slot, _____

7. bunch, crunch, _____

8. sell, bell, _____

Review Lessons 6–10

Some of the spelling words are action words. Write each spelling word next to its meaning.

I. to pull on   _____

2. to fall   _____

3. to hold on to   _____

4. to think ahead   _____

5. to capture   _____

6. to question   _____

Write the missing spelling words.

I. Did you _____ your books home?

2. I will _____ you a letter soon.

3. The truck is _____ in the mud.

4. Which song do you think is the _____?

5. I poured some milk in my _____.

6. Li will _____ to win the race.

7. The roses will _____ in the spring.

8. Turn on the _____ so you can see.

Lesson 11 Words with the Long **a** Sound

Say each word. Listen for the long **a** sound. Write the word.

Spelling Tip	The long **a** sound can be spelled **a-consonant-e**, **ay**, and **ai**. The sign for the long **a** sound is /ā/.

Spelling Words

lake   _____

stay   _____

wait   _____

take   _____

play   _____

came   _____

rain   _____

safe   _____

late   _____

sail   _____

Lesson 11 Words with the Long **a** Sound

Words in Context

Write the missing spelling words.

A Rainy Day

> Challenge
>
> Circle the other words in the story with the /ā/ sound.

I did not want to _____ in today. I was ready to _____ outside. But it was too _____! The sky was gray and _____ was falling. I went inside to make sure I was _____ from the storm. I didn't have to _____ very long before the sun _____ out. I decided to _____ my toy boat outside. I placed it in a puddle so it could _____ like a ship in a _____.

Word Building

Add **ing** to tell what the boys are doing. Then, write the words.

1. The boys play. The boys are play_____. _____
2. The boys sail. The boys are sail_____. _____
3. The boys stay. The boys are stay_____. _____
4. The boys wait. The boys are wait_____. _____

Lesson 11 Words with the Long **a** Sound

Fun with Words

Write the missing letters to make the /ā/ sound in the spelling words.

1. s _____ f _____

2. c _____ m _____

3. w _____ _____ t

4. st _____ _____

5. l _____ t _____

6. r _____ _____ n

7. t _____ k _____

8. pl _____ _____

9. s _____ _____ l

10. l _____ k _____

Words Across the Curriculum

Say each science word. Then, write each word.

1. hay _____

2. taste _____

3. trail _____

4. grape _____

Write each science word next to its definition.

1. to sense the flavor of _____

2. a path in the woods _____

3. food for a horse _____

4. a fruit that grows on a vine _____

Lesson 11 Words with the Long **a** Sound

Words in Writing

Imagine that you are at bat in a baseball game. Write a description of what happens. Use at least three words from the box.

lake	wait	play	rain	late	hay	trail
stay	take	came	safe	sail	bait	grape

_____

_____

_____

_____

Misspelled Words

Read the student's description of part of a baseball game. Circle the six misspelled words. Then, write the words correctly.

I caim up to the plate. The pitcher did not tayke long to throw a fast ball. I swung my bat too laite. Strike one! On the next plae, I cracked the ball hard. I didn't wate to see where the ball landed. I ran to first base. I was saif!

_____   _____   _____

_____   _____   _____

Lesson 12 Words with the Long i Sound

Say each word. Listen for the long **i** sound. Write the word.

Spelling Tip	The long **i** sound can be spelled **i**, **i-consonant-e**, **y**, and **igh**. The sign for the long **i** sound is /ī/.

Spelling Words

cry   _____

pine   _____

light   _____

nice   _____

why   _____

find   _____

right   _____

spy   _____

spider   _____

night   _____

Lesson 12 Words with the Long i Sound

Words in Context
Write the missing spelling words.

Lost in the Woods

Challenge

Circle the other words in the story with the /ī/ sound.

Once, a princess was lost in the woods at _____.

It was so dark that she could not see any _____. The

princess shook with fright. She went to hide under a

_____ tree and began to _____.

Suddenly, she heard a tiny voice.

"_____ are you crying?" asked the voice.

"Who's there?" cried the princess. "Are you

trying to _____ on me?"

"No, I am just a shy _____ who

lives in a web in the woods," said the voice. "I can

help you _____ your way home."

The spider dropped down

_____

in front of the princess. She looked at it for a minute. "That is very

_____ of you," she finally said. " I don't know why so

many people are afraid of spiders."

Lesson 12 Words with the Long i Sound

Fun with Words

Write the spelling word that fits part of each rhyme.

1. The little rabbit might
   go for a hop at _____.

2. That book was so _____
   that I read it twice!

3. I think you will _____
   that it's great to be kind.

4. It is very bright
   when we turn on the _____.

Words Across the Curriculum

Say each math word. Then, write each word.

1. line   _____   3. minus   _____

2. wide   _____   4. pint   _____

Write the missing math words.

1. Nine _____ five equals four.

2. One _____ is half a quart.

3. A straight _____ connects two points.

4. You can measure how _____ a box is.

Lesson 12 Words with the Long i Sound

Words in Writing

Write a fairy tale. Use at least three words from the box.

cry	light	why	right	spider	line	minus
pine	nice	find	spy	night	wide	pint

_____

_____

_____

_____

_____

_____

_____

Dictionary Practice

Circle the word in each set that comes first in ABC order. Then, write it on the line.

1. why went wolf _____

2. cry cup clip _____

3. not new nice _____

4. spy stop soft _____

Lesson 13 Words with the Long o Sound

Say each word. Listen for the long **o** sound. Write the word.

Spelling Tip	The long **o** sound can be spelled **oa**, **o-consonant-e**, and **ow**. The sign for the long **o** sound is /ō/.

Spelling Words

own   _____

coat   _____

woke   _____

flow   _____

toad   _____

row   _____

those   _____

road   _____

slow   _____

float   _____

Lesson 13 Words with the Long o Sound

Words in Context

Write the missing spelling words.

On the River

Aunt Rose has her _____ cabin. Just down the

_____ from her cabin is a river. Aunt Rose takes me

out on the river in her boat. Sometimes, we use paddles to

_____ the boat. When we want to _____

down, we just let the boat _____ and watch the river

_____. Once, I saw a brown _____

sleeping near the river. A flock of crows landed nearby and

_____ up the toad. I hoped _____ crows

would leave it alone. The toad hopped away and hid under a stone.

Word Building

Some words sound the same but have different spellings and meanings.
Write each word from the box next to the word that sounds the same.

hey	sale	rode	rose

1. road _____   3. sail _____

2. rows _____   4. hay _____

Lesson 13 Words with the Long o Sound

Fun with Words

Write the spelling words that complete the rhymes.

1. You can _____ a boat,

   or just let it _____.

2. Did you see the toad by the side of the _____?

3. You can stop or go and move fast or _____.

4. When you are alone, you're on your _____.

5. The water will _____ and make the plants grow.

Words Across the Curriculum

Say each science word. Then, write each word.

1. grow   _____   3. rose   _____

2. soap   _____   4. goat   _____

Write each science word next to its definition.

1. a flower with thorns on its stem   _____

2. to get bigger and older   _____

3. a farm animal that eats grass   _____

4. a bar that makes suds for washing   _____

Lesson 13 Words with the Long o Sound

Words in Writing

Write a paragraph about a person you like to visit. Use at least three of the words from the box.

own	woke	toad	those	slow	grow	rose
coat	flow	row	road	float	soap	goat

_____

_____

_____

_____

_____

Misspelled Words

Circle the word in each set that is spelled correctly. Then, write it on the line.

1. flote   flowt   float   _____

2. owne   own   oan   _____

3. toad   tode   towd   _____

4. floe   flow   flowe   _____

5. row   rowe   roe   _____

6. sloe   slowe   slow   _____

Lesson 14 Words with the /ü/ Sound

Say each word. Listen for the /ü/ sound. Write the word.

| Spelling Tip | The /ü/ sound can be spelled **oo** and **u-consonant-e**. |

Spelling Words

too   _____

rude   _____

room   _____

zoo   _____

glue   _____

soon   _____

cool   _____

moon   _____

food   _____

pool   _____

Lesson 14 Words with the /ü/ Sound

Words in Context

Write the missing spelling words.

Otters

Challenge

Circle the other words in the description with the /ü/ sound.

I like to see otters at the _____. They splash and

fool around in their _____, even when it's

_____ outside. They zoom down their slide, too.

Sometimes, the otters are _____ to each other. One

otter sometimes steals a small piece of _____ from

another otter. Then, it runs into a _____ in their shelter

and hides. The otters play until the _____ comes out at

night. I hope to visit them _____.

Word Building

sun + shine = sunshine

A compound word is made of two smaller
words. Write the spelling word that goes with
each word. Then, write the compound word.

I. bed + _____ = _____

2. _____ + keeper = _____

3. _____ + light = _____

Lesson 14 Words with the /ü/ Sound

Fun with Words

Subtract and add letters to make spelling words.

1. coop – p + l =   _____

2. fool – l + d =   _____

3. rule – l + d =   _____

4. noon – n + s =   _____

5. gloom – oom + ue = _____

6. loom – l + r =   _____

7. moo – m + z =   _____

8. spool – s =   _____

Words Across the Curriculum

Say each art word. Then, write each word.

1. tune   _____

2. tube   _____

Write the missing art words.

3. Paint can come in a jar or a _____.

4. The band played a happy _____.

Lesson 14 Words with the /ü/ Sound

Words in Writing

Write a list of rules for school, home, or another place. Use at least three words from the box.

too	room	glue	cool	food	tune
rude	zoo	soon	moon	pool	tube

_____

_____

_____

_____

Misspelled Words

Read the student's list of rules. Circle the five misspelled words. Then, write the words correctly.

1. Do not run near the poole. _____

2. Keep all fude away from the water. _____

3. Get out of the water as sune as the lifeguards blow their whistles. _____

4. Don't be rood to the lifeguards. _____

5. Keep the dressing rome clean. _____

Lesson 15 Words with the Long **e** Sound

Say each word. Listen for the long **e** sound. Write the word.

Spelling Tip	The long **e** sound can be spelled **e**, **ee** and **ea**. The sign for the long **e** sound is /ē/.

Spelling Words

eat _____

meet _____

team _____

keep _____

each _____

leave _____

read _____

teeth _____

sleep _____

clean _____

Lesson 15 Words with the Long e Sound

Words in Context
Write the missing spelling words.

Saturdays

Saturday is a busy day for me. After I brush my _____

and _____ breakfast, I have to _____

my room. I have to _____ working until it's time for

lunch. After lunch, I _____ my house to go to my

soccer game. I _____ the players on my soccer

_____ at the field. _____ one of us has

to run at least three laps before our game. After we play our game,

I usually go to a movie. Before I go to

_____, I _____

a book and have a cup of hot tea.

Word Building
Add the **-ing** ending to make new words.

1. eat_____   4. keep_____

2. read_____   5. clean_____

3. meet_____   6. sleep_____

Lesson 15 Words with the Long e Sound

Fun with Words

Write the spelling word that fits each sentence and rhymes with each underlined word.

1. We <u>need</u> to _____ a book each week.

2. This group of players <u>seem</u> to be a <u>dream</u> _____.

3. I counted <u>sheep</u> to help me _____.

4. I sat on my <u>seat</u> to _____ my <u>meat</u>.

5. I can <u>reach</u> _____ <u>peach</u> on the tree.

6. Do you <u>greet</u> everyone you _____?

Words Across the Curriculum

Say each math word. Then, write each word.

1. week _____   3. equal _____

2. meter _____   4. even _____

Write the missing math words.

1. Three plus three is _____ to six.

2. A _____ is a metric unit of length.

3. Two, four, and six are _____ numbers.

4. There are seven days in one _____.

Lesson 15 Words with the Long e Sound

Words in Writing

Make a list of things that you do on weekends.
Use at least three words from the box.

eat	team	each	read	sleep	week	equal
meet	keep	leave	teeth	clean	meter	even

_____

_____

_____

_____

Misspelled Words

Read the student's list of things to do. Circle the seven misspelled
words. Then, write the words correctly.

1. Brush my teath.   _____

2. Cleen my room and   _____

   put eech toy away.   _____

3. Practice soccer with the players on my teem. _____

4. Reed a book.   _____

5. Meete my sister for lunch.   _____

6. I will eet a snack with my tea.   _____

Review Lessons 11-15

Write the spelling word that means the opposite of each word.

1. give   _____

2. warm   _____

3. fast   _____

4. dark   _____

5. wake   _____

6. go   _____

7. sink   _____

8. mean   _____

9. day   _____

10. early   _____

Write the spelling word that belongs with each pair of words.

1. pond, river,   _____

2. sob, weep,   _____

3. oak, elm,   _____

4. street, alley,   _____

5. sun, Earth,   _____

6. hat, mittens,   _____

Review Lessons 11–15

Write each spelling word next to the word that means the same.

1. chilly _____

2. wash _____

3. kind _____

4. every _____

5. correct _____

6. save _____

7. go _____

8. also _____

Write the spelling words where they belong.

Today, I am going to _____ my friends at the

beach next to the _____. We will _____

bring some _____ to eat for lunch under a

_____ tree. Then, we'll _____ on the

water. We might also _____ some games in the sand.

I hope it doesn't _____!

Lesson 16 Words with **br** and **fr**

Say each word. Listen to the beginning sound. Write the word.

Spelling Tip	The /br/ and /fr/ sounds are spelled **br** and **fr**.

Spelling Words

free   _____

bright   _____

from   _____

brush   _____

break   _____

frog   _____

broom   _____

fresh   _____

front   _____

bread   _____

Lesson 16 Words with **br** and **fr**

Words in Context

Write the missing spelling words.

A Painting for Frank

Challenge

Circle the other words in the story with **br** and **fr**.

Today, I painted a picture. I used my _____ to

make a _____ yellow sun in a blue sky. Then, I painted

a brown tree with leaves falling _____ its branches. In

_____ of the tree, I painted a green

_____. Then, my friend Frank asked me if I wanted to

take a _____. We ate some _____ and

_____ fruit. Frank swept up the crumbs with a

_____. When I finished my painting,

I gave it to Frank for _____.

Word Building

A compound word is made of two smaller words. Write the spelling
word that goes with each word. Then, write the compound word.

1. _____ + fast = _____

2. _____ + crumb = _____

3. paint + _____ = _____

4. _____ + stick = _____

Lesson 16 Words with **br** and **fr**

Fun with Words

Write the spelling words that complete the comparisons.

1. **Dig** is to **shovel** as **sweep** is to _____.

2. **Dark** is to **night** as _____ is to **light**.

3. **Crayon** is to **color** as _____ is to **paint**.

4. **Top** is to **bottom** as _____ is to **back**.

5. **Open** is to **close** as _____ is to **trap**.

6. **Snake** is to **slither** as _____ is to **hop**.

Words Across the Curriculum

Say each science word. Then, write each word.

1. frost _____   3. fruit _____

2. brick _____   4. breeze _____

Write each science word next to the pair of words it belongs with.

1. stone, wood, _____

2. apple, orange, _____

3. snow, ice, _____

4. wind, air, _____

Lesson 16 Words with **br** and **fr**

Words in Writing

Write a paragraph that tells about an animal.
Use at least three of the words from the box.

free	from	break	broom	front	frost	fruit
bright	brush	frog	fresh	bread	brick	breeze

_____

_____

_____

_____

_____

Misspelled Words

Read the student's description of an animal. Circle the four
misspelled words. Then, write the words correctly.

    I found a frogg at the pond. I named him Freddie. Freddie's skin is
brite green. He has brown spots on the frunt of his legs. I decided not
to take Freddie from the pond. Freddie needs to be free. He likes to
sit by the pond and feel the breze on his skin.

_____   _____

_____   _____

Lesson 17 Words with sl and sp

Say each word. Listen to the beginning sound. Write the word.

Spelling Tip	The /sl/ and /sp/ sounds are spelled sl and sp.

Spelling Words

spin   _____

slip   _____

slam   _____

sled   _____

speak   _____

slide   _____

sport   _____

spill   _____

spoon   _____

slice   _____

Lesson 17 Words with **sl** and **sp**

Words in Context

Write the missing spelling words.

Winter Fun

Challenge

Circle the other words in the description with **sl** and **sp**.

In winter, I like to speed down a snowy hill on my

_____. I go so fast, I can't stop to _____

to my friends who are on the slope. Ice-skating is another fun winter

_____. Sometimes, I _____ in a circle on

the ice. Then, I _____ on the ice as fast as I can. I try

not to _____ into other skaters. When I go over a slick

spot on the ice, sometimes I _____ and fall. When I get

too cold, I go inside. I have a _____ of pizza and a

bowl of hot soup. My hands are so cold I have to

grip my _____ so I don't

_____ my soup.

Word Building

Write the word from the box that tells about the past.

1. Today, I **spin**. Yesterday, I _____.

2. Today, I **speak**. Yesterday, I _____.

spoke
spun

Lesson 17 Words with **sl** and **sp**

Fun with Words

Fill in the missing vowels to make the spelling words.

1. sp_____ _____n   6. sl_____c_____

2. sl_____d   7. sl_____p

3. sl_____d_____   8. sp_____rt

4. sp_____ll   9. sp_____ _____k

5. sl_____m   10. sp_____n

Words Across the Curriculum

Say each art word. Then, write each word.

1. slant   _____   3. space   _____

2. slit   _____   4. spray   _____

Write the missing art words.

1. You can brush or _____ paint on a work of art.

2. Zigzag lines _____ from one side to another.

3. To make a mask, cut one _____ for each eye.

4. It's good to leave some empty _____ in a painting.

Lesson 17 Words with **sl** and **sp**

Words in Writing

Write about what you like to do outside in winter. Use at least three of the words from the box.

spin	slam	speak	sport	spoon	slant	space
slip	sled	slide	spill	slice	slit	spray

_____

_____

_____

_____

_____

_____

Dictionary Practice

To find a word in a dictionary, you sometimes have to look at the second letter of the words on a page. Circle the second letter in each word. Then, write the words in ABC order.

1. slide	5. sweep	1. _____	5. _____
2. stick	6. skip	2. _____	6. _____
3. show	7. spin	3. _____	7. _____
4. small	8. snake	4. _____	8. _____

Lesson 18 Words with **sh** and **wh**

Say each word. Listen to the beginning sound. Write the word.

Spelling Tip	The /sh/ and /wh/ sounds are often spelled **sh** and **wh**.

Spelling Words

whip   _____

shoe   _____

shall   _____

wheel   _____

share   _____

shine   _____

while   _____

shake   _____

where   _____

which   _____

Lesson 18 Words with **sh** and **wh**

Words in Context

Write the missing spelling words.

What to Do?

> **Challenge**
>
> Circle the other words in the story with **sh** and **wh**.

It rained all morning. The sun wasn't going to

_____ all day. "What _____

I do today?" I asked my mom.

"You can help me make a cake," she said.

"_____ should I start?" I asked.

"You can _____ the egg whites," Mom said. She gave

me a tool with a small _____ on top. She showed me

_____ way to turn it. As I mixed the eggs into the

batter, I spilled a little bit on my _____.

_____ the cake was baking, Mom made a chocolate

_____ for us to _____.

Word Building

Add **s** to each word to mean more than one. Then, write the word.

1. one shoe, two shoe_____   _____

2. one sport, two sport_____   _____

3. one wheel, two wheel_____   _____

Lesson 18   Words with **sh** and **wh**

Fun with Words

Unscramble the letters to make the spelling words.

1. lashl   _____   6. phiw   _____

2. sneih   _____   7. rheas   _____

3. ekahs   _____   8. lhewi   _____

4. ehwer   _____   9. elweh   _____

5. oesh   _____   10. ciwhh   _____

Words Across the Curriculum

Say each science word. Then, write each word.

1. shore   _____   3. shadow _____

2. wheat   _____   4. shade   _____

Write the science word next to the place in which you can find it.

1. in a field   _____

2. under a tree   _____

3. behind you   _____

4. next to a lake   _____

Lesson 18 Words with **sh** and **wh**

Words in Writing

What kind of party would you like to have?
Write an invitation to a party. Use at least
three of the words from the box.

whip	shall	share	while	where	shore	shadow
shoe	wheel	shine	shade	which	wheat	shade

_____

_____

_____

_____

_____

Misspelled Words

Read the invitation. Circle the five misspelled words. Then, write the
words correctly on the lines below.

When: 2:00 on Saturday, May 3, rain or shene
Wheer: At the park near the shoar of the lake
Given by: Mia

P.S. Please bring a snack to sheare. I shal bring everything else.

_____   _____   _____

_____   _____

Lesson 19 Words with ch and th

Say each word. Listen for the **ch** and **th** sounds. Write the word.

Spelling Tip	The /ch/ and /th/ sounds are often spelled **ch** and **th**.

Spelling Words

with   _____

such   _____

think   _____

both   _____

chase   _____

reach   _____

thing   _____

teach   _____

catch   _____

child   _____

Lesson 19 Words with **ch** and **th**

Words in Context

Write the missing spelling words.

Soccer Is Fun!

> **Challenge**
>
> Circle the other words in the story with **ch** and **th**.

Do you like to play soccer? It's _____ a fun sport! I

_____ that every _____ should learn

how to play. Most coaches _____ their players to kick

and trap the ball with _____ feet. They also tell the

players to stay in their positions and not _____ the ball

all over the field. Another _____ players have to

remember is not to _____ for the ball

_____ their hands. Only the goalkeeper can use his

hands to _____ the ball.

Word Building

Add **er** to each word below to make a word
that names a person who does an action.

1. catch + er = _____

2. play + er = _____

3. read + er = _____

4. think + er = _____

Lesson 19 Words with **ch** and **th**

Fun with Words

Add **ch** or **th** to make the spelling words that rhyme.

1. match, cat_____   5. wild, _____ild

2. base, _____ase   6. much, su_____

3. ring, _____ing   7. pink, _____ink

4. peach, rea_____   8. beach, tea_____

Words Across the Curriculum

Say each math word. Then, write each word.

1. inch _____   3. change _____

2. month _____   4. width _____

Write each math word next to the word it is like.

1. money   _____

2. distance across   _____

3. length   _____

4. week   _____

Lesson 19 Words with **ch** and **th**

Words in Writing

What is your favorite sport? Write a paragraph that tells how to play the sport. Use at least three of the words from the box.

_____

_____

_____

_____

with	think	chase	thing	catch	inch	change
such	both	reach	teach	child	month	width

Dictionary Practice

A dictionary has guide words at the top of the page. All the words on the page come between the guide words in ABC order. Write the word from the box that comes between each pair of guide words.

1. wash   _____   wise

2. take   _____   thing

3. bath   _____   bring

4. ship   _____   swim

5. race   _____   rich

Review Lessons 16–19

Write the spelling word that has the same meaning.

1. turn   _____

2. shiver   _____

3. grab   _____

4. glow   _____

5. cut   _____

6. will   _____

7. game   _____

8. beat   _____

Write the spelling word that rhymes with each pair of words.

1. log, fog,   _____

2. jam, dam,   _____

3. make, rake,   _____

4. moon, noon,   _____

5. meal, peel,   _____

6. light, night, _____

7. ride, hide,   _____

8. beak, week,   _____

Review Lessons 16–19

Write the spelling word that means the opposite.

1. dull _____

2. throw _____

3. back _____

4. fix _____

5. to _____

6. capture _____

Write the spelling words that fit the questions.

1. _____ are you going?

2. Did you sweep the floor with the _____?

3. Did you hear the door _____?

4. Can I _____ your hair for you?

5. _____ book should we read?

6. Would you like to _____ my lunch with me?

7. May I have some jam on my _____?

8. Can I ride your _____ down the hill?

Lesson 20 Words with the /är/ Sound

Say each word. Listen for the /är/ sound. Write the word.

Spelling Tip	The /är/ sound is often spelled **ar**.

Spelling Words

far   _____

farm   _____

yard   _____

cart   _____

hard   _____

park   _____

start   _____

part   _____

sharp   _____

garden   _____

Lesson 20 Words with the /är/ Sound

Words in Context

Write the missing spelling words.

Farm Work

There is a lot of _____ work to do on a

_____. You have to set your alarm early and then

_____ working. First, you feed the animals. Then, you

let them out of the barn. You have to make sure they don't go

_____ from the _____. This is only

_____ of the day's work. There are more chores

outside in the _____. You have to dig up weeds with a

_____ tool. Then, you wheel them away

in a _____. It's much harder to work

on a farm than in a _____!

Word Building

The ending **-er** can compare two things. Add **er** to make a new word
that compares. Then, write the new word.

1. This tack is **sharp**. That tack is **sharp**_____.   _____

2. This job is **hard**. That job is **hard**_____.   _____

3. This dog is **smart**. That dog is **smart**_____.   _____

Lesson 20 Words with the /är/ Sound

Fun with Words

Write the spelling word that completes each rhyme.

1. Don't let the dog bark when he runs in the _____.

2. It's not very hard to work in the _____.

3. It's time to _____ on a work of art.

4. An actor who's smart will play a good _____.

5. You can go very _____ when you drive in a car.

6. You must have a strong arm to work on a _____.

Words Across the Curriculum

Say each art word. Then, write each word.

1. art   _____   **3.** carve   _____

2. dark   _____   **4.** mark   _____

Write the art words to complete the directions.

Here's how to make a jack o'lantern from a pumpkin. First, use

a _____ pen to _____ the parts of the

face. Then, have an adult use a knife to _____ them

out. If you do a good job, you will have a work of _____!

Lesson 20 Words with the /är/ Sound

Words in Writing

Have you ever had a dog for a pet? Write a
list of things to do to take care of a dog. Use
at least three of the words from the box.

far	yard	hard	start	sharp	art	carve
farm	cart	park	part	garden	dart	mark

_____

_____

_____

_____

_____

Misspelled Words

Read the list of things to do to take care of a dog. Circle the five
misspelled words. Then, write the words correctly.

1. Let the dog play in the yerd. _____

2. Don't let her dig in the gerden. _____

3. Cut her nails when they start to get too sharpe. _____

4. Take her for walks in the parck. _____

5. Don't let her get too fare away. _____

Lesson 21 Words with the /ôr/ and /ûr/ Sounds

Say each word. Listen for the /ôr/ and /ûr/ sounds. Write the word.

Spelling Tip	The /ôr/ sound can be spelled **ir** or **ur**. The /ûr/ sound can be spelled **or**.

Spelling Words

girl   _____

fort   _____

turn   _____

first   _____

more   _____

hurt   _____

dirt   _____

store   _____

short   _____

burn   _____

Lesson 21 Words with the /ôr/ and /ûr/ Sounds

Words in Context

Write the missing spelling words.

Challenge

Circle the other words in the letter with the /ôr/ and /ûr/ sounds.

Dear Burt,

Thank you for letting me stay

at your farm last weekend. Now, it's your _____ to visit

me. We can shop at the new sports _____. It's just a

_____ walk down the street. We also can play with the

_____ who lives next door. She and I just built a

_____ in her yard. _____, we collected

some boards that her dad didn't need. He was going to

_____ them in the fireplace. We nailed the boards

together to make the fort. I _____ my finger with the

hammer, but it's not too sore. We packed the _____

down hard to make a floor. I'll tell you _____ about the

fort the next time I write.

Your friend,
Mario

Lesson 21 Words with the /ôr/ and /ûr/ Sounds

Fun with Words

Write the spelling word that completes each tongue-twister.

1. Steve's _____ still sells stickers.

2. Dad doesn't dig _____ during the day.

3. Tim took a _____ telling a tall tale.

4. Mary must make _____ money.

5. Greta is a _____ who gets good grades.

6. Sue shall show Shellie the six _____ sheep.

Words Across the Curriculum

Say each science word. Then, write each word.

1. bird _____   3. north _____

2. horse _____   4. turtle _____

Write each science word next to the group of words it belongs with.

1. south, east, west, _____

2. lizard, snake, alligator, _____

3. zebra, mule, pony, _____

4. robin, eagle, owl, _____

Lesson 21 Words with the /ôr/ and /ûr/ Sounds

Words in Writing

Write the directions to a place near your home. Use at least three words from the box.

girl	turn	more	dirt	short	bird	north
fort	first	hurt	store	burn	horse	turtle

_____

_____

_____

_____

_____

Misspelled Words

Circle the correct spelling for each word.

1. furst   forst   first   _____

2. hurt   hirt   hort   _____

3. store   stor   sture   _____

4. tirn   turn   turne   _____

5. shurt   short   shirte   _____

6. burn   birn   burne   _____

Lesson 22 Words with c and s

Say each word. Listen for the /s/ and /z/ sounds. Write the word.

Spelling Tip	The /s/ sound can be spelled **s** or **ce**. The /z/ sound can be spelled **se**.

Spelling Words

once _____

use _____

race _____

nose _____

nice _____

please _____

mouse _____

place _____

house _____

because _____

Lesson 22 Words with c and s

Words in Context

Write the missing spelling words.

My Pet Mike

I have a pet _____ named Mike. He has a gray

body with white spots on his face. He also has a long, pointed

_____. At first, my mom didn't want him in the

_____. I had to beg her to _____ let me

keep Mike. When she saw how _____ he is, my mom

said yes. _____, Mike got loose _____ I

forgot to close his cage door. I had to _____ after him.

He ran all over the _____.

I finally chased him into a corner. Then,

I had to _____ a net to

catch him. It's a good thing my mom

wasn't home!

Lesson 22 Words with c and s

Fun with Words

Add **se** or **ce** to make the spelling words.

1. hou _____

2. becau _____

3. no _____

4. ra _____

5. u _____

6. ni _____

7. mou _____

8. on _____

9. pla _____

10. plea _____

Words Across the Curriculum

Say each art word. Then, write each word.

1. dance _____

2. pose _____

3. pencil _____

4. paste _____

Write the art word that completes each sentence.

1. Will you _____ for me so I can paint a picture of you?

2. I used a _____ to sketch the house.

3. It's fun to sing and _____.

4. You can _____ cutout shapes on a sheet of paper.

Lesson 22 Words with c and s

Words in Writing

Write a description of a piece of art you made. Use at least three of the words from the box.

once	race	nice	mouse	house	dance	pencil
use	nose	please	place	because	pose	paste

_____

_____

_____

_____

Dictionary Practice

A dictionary has a beginning, middle, and end. Write ten spelling words where you would find them in the dictionary.

ABCDEFGH   **IJKLMNOPQ**   **RSTUVWXYZ**

_____   _____   _____

_____   _____   _____

                    _____

                    _____

                    _____

                    _____

Review Lessons 20–22

Write the spelling word that means the opposite.

1. easy _____

2. last _____

3. tall _____

4. boy _____

5. stop _____

6. dull _____

7. less _____

8. mean _____

9. near _____

10. whole _____

Write the spelling word that names a place where you would find each thing.

1. flowers _____

2. bedroom _____

3. soldiers _____

4. crops _____

Review Lessons 20–22

Write the spelling word that tells about each action.

1. You can _____ a car in a lot.

2. You can _____ a pencil to draw a picture.

3. You can _____ with other runners.

4. You can _____ your finger on a hot stove.

Write the spelling word that completes each sentence.

1. I stayed in bed today _____ I was sick.

2. Go down the hall and _____ left at the second door.

3. May I _____ see your new book?

4. I like to play with my friends at the _____.

5. My mom pushed the shopping _____ through the store.

6. Did you _____ your foot when you stepped on the tack?

7. My cat chased a _____ in the yard.

8. _____, I saw a shooting star in the sky.

Lesson 23 Words with the Endings –s and -es

Say each word. Look at the two letters before the **–s** or **–es** ending. Write the word.

Spelling Tip	Add **s** or **es** to most nouns to mean more than one. When a word ends with **s**, **ss**, **ch**, **sh** or **x**, add **es**.

Spelling Words

students   _____

foxes   _____

bushes   _____

watches   _____

beaches   _____

branches   _____

classes   _____

books   _____

flashes   _____

animals   _____

Lesson 23 Words with the Endings -s and -es

Words in Context

Write the missing spelling words.

A Fun Day

Yesterday, the _____ at our school had a fun day.

We didn't stay in our rooms, and we didn't read any

_____. We didn't have any _____ at all.

Instead, we rode in buses to the lake.

We rode past a few _____

before we stopped to go swimming. We

changed our clothes and took off our

_____. We left them under some _____

and went swimming. After a few hours, it started to rain. We saw

some _____ of lightning behind some tree

_____. Soon, the rain stopped. We hiked through the

forest by the lake to look for _____. We saw a lot of

birds and squirrels. We even saw two red _____.

Lesson 23 Words with the Endings -s and -es

Fun with Words
Circle the hidden spelling words.

```
t  b  r  a  n  c  h  e  s  t  e
o  c  l  t  o  l  r  x  e  b  s
s  b  u  c  r  m  p  s  n  b  t
k  f  w  r  l  g  o  p  c  u  u
c  l  o  a  n  i  m  a  l  s  d
e  a  f  o  x  e  s  a  a  h  e
h  s  a  n  b  o  o  k  s  e  n
p  h  w  a  t  c  h  e  s  s  t
b  e  r  o  j  s  s  m  e  m  s
a  s  b  e  a  c  h  e  s  c  e
```

Words Across the Curriculum

Say each social studies word. Then, write each word.

1. states _____   3. friends _____

2. speeches _____   4. signs _____

Write the social studies word that completes each sentence.

1. Traffic _____ tell you what to do.

2. People give _____ to tell about something they know.

3. Our _____ play with us and help us.

4. There are 50 _____ in our country.

Lesson 23 Words with the Endings -s and -es

Words in Writing

Write a paragraph that tells what you do on the weekends. Use at least three words from the box.

students	bushes	beaches	classes	flashes	states	friends
foxes	watches	branches	books	animals	speeches	signs

_____

_____

_____

_____

Misspelled Words

Read the paragraph. Circle the four misspelled words. Then, write the words correctly on the lines below.

On the weekends, there are no school clases. I help my dad clean our house. I also help him cut the grass and trim the buches in the yard. We leave some food out for the wild animals. Then, I play outside with my friendes. When we get tired, we go inside and read bookes.

_____   _____

_____   _____

Lesson 24 Words with the Endings -ed and -ing

Say each word. Listen to the ending sound. Write the word.

Spelling Tip	For some words with only one vowel, double the last consonant before adding **ed** or **ing**.

Spelling Words

winning _____

tapped _____

clapping _____

digging _____

slipped _____

stepped _____

running _____

dropped _____

skipped _____

hugged _____

NAME _____

Lesson 24 Words with the Endings -ed and -ing

Words in Context

Write the missing spelling words.

The Last Inning

Circle the other words in the story that have double consonants before **ed** or **ing**.

The baseball game was in

the last inning. The Tigers' best batter was next. He _____

up to the plate. He looked down and started _____

the toe of his shoe into the dirt. Then he looked up at the pitcher and

gripped his bat with both hands. He gently _____ the

first pitch with his bat and started _____ to first base.

The ball popped out to left field. The outfielder held out his mitt, but

then his feet _____ on the wet grass. He

_____ the ball! The runner on third

base _____ to home plate. The other

players on his team ran out and _____

him. The fans started _____ and

hopping up and down. The Tigers still had their

_____ streak.

Spectrum Spelling
Grade 2

Lesson 24
Words with the Endings -ed and -ing
109

Lesson 24 Words with the Endings -ed and -ing

Fun with Words

Write the spelling word that rhymes with the underlined word and fits in each sentence.

1. I _____ the chips that I had <u>chopped</u>.

2. The _____ players were all <u>grinning</u>.

3. I <u>tripped</u> and fell as I _____ down the road.

4. The fans were _____ and <u>tapping</u> their feet.

5. The baby's mom _____ him when he <u>tugged</u> on her dress.

6. The stick <u>snapped</u> in two when I _____ it on the floor.

Words Across the Curriculum

Say each art word. Then, write each word.

1. cutting _____   3. dipped _____

2. hummed _____   4. dripping _____

Write the missing art words.

1. Some people make artwork by _____ paint onto paper.

2. Be careful when you're _____ paper with scissors.

3. I _____ my brush into the blue paint.

4. The boy _____ a tune to himself.

Lesson 24 Words with the Endings -ed and -ing

Words in Writing

What sport do you like to watch? Write a
description of a sports game you watched.
Use at least three words from the box.

| winning | tapped | clapping | digging | slipped | cutting | dipped |
| stepped | running | dropped | skipped | hugged | hummed | dripping |

_____

_____

_____

_____

Misspelled Words

Read the description. Circle the five misspelled words. Then, write the
words correctly.

I like to watch my dad play basketball. I don't care if his team is
wining or losing. In his last game, he scored 10 points. Everyone was
claping when his shots dipped into the basket. Near the end of the
game, he slippet and fell. He dropt the ball. Another player steped
on his hand, but he wasn't hurt. I hugged him after the game.

_____   _____   _____

_____   _____

Lesson 25 Easily Misspelled Words

Say each word. Look at the spelling. Write the word.

Spelling Tip	Some words aren't spelled the way they sound. You have to remember how to spell them.

Spelling Words

our   _____

give   _____

very   _____

new   _____

were   _____

goes   _____

many   _____

next   _____

why   _____

every   _____

Lesson 25 Easily Misspelled Words

Words in Context

Write the missing spelling words.

Yard Sale

Challenge

Circle the three words in the ad that have a **vowel-consonant-e** pattern but a short vowel sound.

Our class is having a yard

sale _____ week. We will have _____ toys

and clothes that _____ used only once or twice. We'll

also have some _____ ones. _____ item

will have a _____ low price. We'll _____

you free cookies and juice just for coming to _____ sale.

The sale _____

on all day. _____

don't you plan to come?

Word Building

Add **s** to each pronoun to show that something belongs to a person or animal. Then, write the word.

1. This is our house. This house is our_____.   _____

2. The dog is happy. It is wagging it_____ tail.   _____

3. Rosa found her coat. That coat is her_____.   _____

4. Is this your pencil? I think it is your_____.   _____

Lesson 25 Easily Misspelled Words

Fun with Words

Write the spelling word that fits in each pattern.

1. go, _____, going

5. is, are, _____

2. one, few, _____, most

6. my, your, _____

3. each, all, _____

7. _____, used, old

4. first, _____, last

8. who, what, _____

Words Across the Curriculum

Say each math word. Then, write each word.

1. cube _____

3. length _____

2. money _____

4. circle _____

Write the math word that completes each sentence.

1. Inches and meters measure _____.

2. A _____ is a closed, curved line.

3. _____ is used to buy things.

4. Most blocks have the shape of a _____.

Lesson 25 Easily Misspelled Words

Words in Writing

Write the words for a poster that tell about a yard sale. Use at least three words from the box.

our	very	were	many	why	cube	length
give	new	goes	next	every	money	circle

_____

_____

_____

_____

_____

Dictionary Practice

Circle the word that comes between each pair of guide words in ABC order.

1. orange—our   oven   open   otter

2. were—who   why   when   woke

3. under—wait   stop   way   very

4. many—most   milk   must   my

5. next—now   napkin   night   nest

6. circle—cry   cube   come   cuddle

Review Lessons 23–25

Write the spelling word that rhymes with each word.

1. stopped _____

2. boxes _____

3. live _____

4. try _____

5. looks _____

6. tugged _____

7. rapped _____

8. dashes _____

9. berry _____

10. glasses _____

Write the spelling word that means the opposite.

1. losing _____

2. none _____

3. old _____

4. few _____

Review Lessons 23–25

Write the spelling word that means the same or almost the same.

1. shores _____

2. walked _____

3. slid _____

4. clocks _____

5. each _____

6. shrubs _____

Write the spelling word that completes each sentence.

1. You can see _____ at the zoo.

2. The girls _____ there when I got home.

3. The birds are sitting on the _____ of the tree.

4. The fans are _____ for their team.

5. I am the _____ person in line.

6. My dog is _____ a hole in the yard.

Lesson 26 Words That Sound the Same

Say each word. Notice the different spellings of the words that sound the same. Write each word.

| Spelling Tip | Some words sound the same but have different spellings and meanings. |

Spelling Words

meat   _____

deer   _____

hole   _____

road   _____

dear   _____

there   _____

whole   _____

meet   _____

rode   _____

their   _____

Lesson 26 Words That Sound the Same

Words in Context

Write the missing spelling words.

_____ Mom,

    I'm having a great time at

Uncle Pete's ranch. Yesterday, we

_____ horses along a dirt _____. We

were on our way to _____ some friends of Uncle Pete.

_____ ranch is only a few miles away. On the way

_____, I saw a _____ hiding in the trees.

It tripped over a _____ in the ground as it ran away.

When we got to the ranch, Uncle Pete and I had lunch. I ate a

_____ plate of _____ and vegetables. I'll

write again soon.

Love,
Irene

> ### Challenge
>
> Circle the words in the letter that sound the same as the words **eye**, **sum**, **too**, **right**, **hour**, **peat**, and **grate**.

Word Building

Add **er** and **est** to make new words that compare.

1. dear, dear_____, dear_____

2. long, long_____, long_____

Lesson 26 Words That Sound the Same

Fun with Words

Write the spelling word that rhymes and has the same spelling pattern.

1. code _____   4. near _____

2. seat _____   5. load _____

3. where _____   6. mole _____

Words Across the Curriculum

Say each science word. Then, write each word.

1. sea _____   3. eye _____

2. hear _____   4. hour _____

Write the science word next to its definition. Then, write a word that sounds the same but has a different spelling and meaning. Use the dictionary in the back if you need help.

1. listen _____   _____

2. 60 minutes _____   _____

3. ocean _____   _____

4. body part that

  lets you see _____   _____

Lesson 26 Words That Sound the Same

Words in Writing

Write an ad for a restaurant where you like to eat. Use at least three words from the box.

meat	hole	dear	whole	rode	sea	eye
deer	road	there	meet	their	hear	hour

_____

_____

_____

_____

_____

Incorrect Words

Read the ad. Circle the six words that are used incorrectly for their meaning. Then, write the correct words.

   Did you here about Mia's Place yet? You can get great food their. You can get a hole pizza for just five dollars. You can get meet or vegetable toppings for free. It's a fun place to meat your friends. It's right on the beach, next to the see.

_____   _____   _____

_____   _____   _____

Lesson 27 Family Words

Say each word. Look at the spelling of each word. Write each word.

Spelling Tip	Many family words don't fit a spelling pattern. You have to remember how to spell them.

Spelling Words

family   _____

mother   _____

father   _____

sister   _____

brother   _____

baby   _____

aunt   _____

uncle   _____

grandfather _____

grandmother _____

Lesson 27 Family Words

Words in Context

Write the missing spelling words.

My Family

> **Challenge**
> Circle the other family words in the description.

There are many people in my _____. My

_____ is a teacher. His parents are my grandparents.

My _____ likes to go fishing in his boat. My

_____ is a very good cook. My _____

is an artist. Sometimes, she paints pictures of me with my

_____ Maria and my _____ Carlos. My

mother's brother is an artist, too. He is my _____. His

wife is my _____. Uncle Paul and Aunt Rita just had a

_____. I like to hold my new cousin.

Lesson 27 Family Words

Fun with Words

Write the spelling word that goes with each clue.

1. your mom _____

2. a girl whose mom is your mom _____

3. your dad _____

4. your dad's brother _____

5. your dad's sister _____

6. a boy whose dad is your dad _____

7. your dad's dad _____

8. your mom's mom _____

Words Across the Curriculum

Say each social studies word. Then, write each word.

1. parent _____ 3. together_____

2. cousin _____ 4. people _____

Write the social studies word or words that complete each sentence.

1. The _____ in a family work and play

_____.

2. A _____ takes care of his or her children.

3. My aunt's son is my _____.

Lesson 27 Family Words

Words in Writing

A family tree shows how the people in a family are related. Make your family tree. Use words from the box to name your family members.

_____

_____

family	father	brother	aunt	grandfather	parent	together
mother	sister	baby	uncle	grandmother	cousin	people

Dictionary Practice

A dictionary has a beginning, middle, and end. Write the words from the box where you would find them in the dictionary.

ABCDEFGH　　　　**IJKLMNOPQ**　　　　**RSTUVWXYZ**

_____　　_____　　_____

_____　　_____　　_____

_____　　_____　　_____

_____

_____

_____

Lesson 28 Number Words

Say each word. Look at the spelling of each word. Write each word.

Spelling Tip	Some number words are spelled the way they sound. You have to remember how to spell others.

Spelling Words

one _____

two _____

three _____

four _____

five _____

six _____

seven _____

eight _____

nine _____

ten _____

Lesson 28 Number Words

Words in Context

Write the missing spelling words.

1. A person has _____ fingers on one hand.

2. A person has _____ fingers altogether.

3. _____ gloves are a pair.

4. There are _____ players on a baseball team.

5. A triangle has _____ sides.

6. The 50 states make _____ country.

7. There are _____ days in a week.

8. A square has _____ sides.

9. A cube has _____ faces.

10. A spider has _____ legs.

Word Building

Some number words add **th** to make words that tell what order things are in. Add **th** to the end of each word to make a new word that tells about order. Then, write the word.

1. four_____   _____

2. six_____   _____

3. seven_____   _____

4. ten_____   _____

Lesson 28 Number Words

Fun with Words

Write the spelling word that rhymes with the underlined word.

1. _____ pigs are in a <u>pen</u>.

2. _____ geese are at the <u>gate</u>.

3. _____ sisters pick up <u>sticks</u>.

4. _____ friends are at the <u>door</u>.

5. _____ bees are in their <u>hive</u>.

6. _____ foxes are running <u>free</u>.

7. _____ circles are colored <u>blue</u>.

8. _____ numbers are on the <u>line</u>.

Words Across the Curriculum

Say each math word. Then, write each word.

1. second _____   3. fifth _____

2. third _____   4. ninth _____

Write the math words in the correct order.

1. first, _____, _____, fourth

2. _____, sixth, seventh

3. eighth, _____, tenth

Lesson 28 Number Words

Words in Writing

Write a paragraph that tells about people in your family. Use at least three words from the box.

one	three	five	seven	nine	second	fifth
two	four	six	eight	ten	third	ninth

_____

_____

_____

_____

_____

_____

Misspelled Words

Read the paragraph. Circle the five misspelled words. Then, write the words correctly.

   I am eigth years old. I'm in the sicond grade. I have one older sister. She is nin years old. She's in the therd grade. I also have two brothers. My older brother is tene. My other brother is just a baby.

_____   _____   _____

_____   _____

Review Lessons 26–28

Write the spelling word that fits each meaning.

1. A brown _____ ran into the woods.

2. I like soup with vegetables and _____.

3. My dog is digging a _____ in the dirt.

4. I will _____ my sister after school.

5. We _____ our bikes home.

6. My brother and I ate a _____ pizza.

7. There are many cars on the _____ today.

8. The boys took off _____ coats.

9. _____ is a pear tree in my yard.

10. My dad's mom is my _____.

Write the spelling word or words that belong with each word.

1. parents   _____   _____

2. grandparents   _____   _____

3. sister   _____

4. aunt   _____

Review Lessons 26–28

Write the spelling word that tells how many.

1.

_____

2.

_____

3.

_____

4.

_____

5.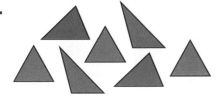

_____

6.

_____

7.

_____

8.

_____

9.

_____

10.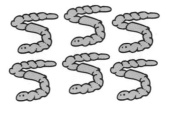

_____

LESSONS 26–28 REVIEW

Lesson 29 Words with the / u̇ / Sound

Say each word. Listen to the /u̇/ sound. Write each word.

Spelling Tip	The /u̇/ sound is often spelled **oo** or **u**.

Spelling Words

look   _____

put   _____

cook   _____

wood   _____

took   _____

full   _____

hook   _____

good   _____

book   _____

stood   _____

Lesson 29 Words with the /ù/ Sound

Words in Context

Write the missing spelling words.

My mom likes to

_____.

She makes cookies and meats.

She doesn't _____

in a _____,

when she whips up her treats.

She has a small nook

that is _____ of her tools.

And hung from a _____,

A list of kitchen rules:

"_____ all dishes away.

Sweep up the _____ floors.

If you've done all the chores,

I will have a _____ day."

I once _____ a turn.

I _____ in her place.

But the food started to burn.

There was smoke everyplace.

Lesson 29 Words with the /u̇/ Sound

Fun with Words

Write the spelling word that completes each tongue-twister.

1. Cara can _____ corn on the cob.

2. Pat _____ a plum on Paul's plate.

3. Tara _____ ten turns trying to tell time.

4. Stan stopped and _____ still.

5. _____ at Len's little lamb.

6. Hank hung his hat on a _____.

Words Across the Curriculum

Say each science word. Then, write each word.

1. push _____   3. wool _____

2. pull _____   4. brook _____

Write the spelling word or words that complete each sentence.

1. A _____ is a creek, or small stream.

2. _____ is made from sheep's hair.

3. A force can be a _____ or a _____.

Lesson 29 Words with the /u̇/ Sound

Words in Writing

Write a list that tells what chores you do at home. Use at least three of the words from the box.

look	cook	took	hook	book	push	wool
put	wood	full	good	stood	pull	brook

_____

_____

_____

_____

_____

Dictionary Practice

Some words have more than one meaning. A dictionary tells when a word is a noun, a verb, or both. Write the five spelling words and science words that can be a noun and a verb.

I took one **step**.
I will **step** over the puddle.

1. _____   3. _____   5. _____

2. _____   4. _____

Lesson 30 Words with the /ou/ Sound

Say each word. Listen for the /ou/ sound. Write each word.

Spelling Tip	The /ou/ sound can be spelled **ou** or **ow**.

Spelling Words

out   _____

owl   _____

now   _____

loud   _____

count   _____

down   _____

sound   _____

south   _____

ground   _____

around   _____

Lesson 30 Words with the /ou/ Sound

Words in Context

Write the missing spelling words.

Gone for the Winter

_____ that it is almost winter, many birds will

fly _____. If you look _____ your window,

you might see some of them. So many birds fly together that you

can't _____ them. This helps to protect them from

bigger birds, such as an eagle or an _____. These big

birds can swoop _____ on smaller birds without making

a _____. The birds fly for many hours before they land

on the _____ to rest. After they rest, some birds make

_____ sounds. The other birds gather

_____ them. All the birds fly off together again.

Lesson 30 Words with the /ou/ Sound

Fun with Words

Use the clues to complete the puzzle with spelling words.

Down

1. opposite of north

3. opposite of up

5. bird with big eyes

7. opposite of in

Across

2. noise

4. at this time

6. opposite of quiet

8. find out how many

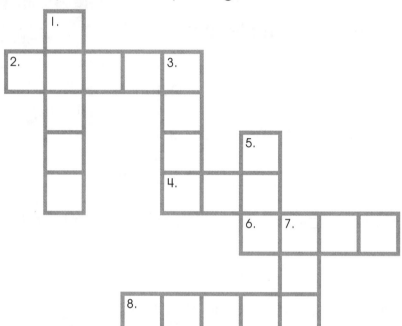

Words Across the Curriculum

Say each social studies word. Then, write each word.

1. town _____   **3.** found _____

2. crowd _____   **4.** crown _____

Write the social studies word that completes each sentence.

1. A king sometimes wears a _____.

2. A _____ is smaller than a city.

3. A _____ of people was there to hear the band.

4. A girl on my street _____ my lost dog.

Lesson 30 Words with the /ou/ Sound

Words in Writing

Write a short report about an animal. Use at least three of the words from the box.

out	now	count	sound	ground	town	found
owl	loud	down	south	around	crowd	crown

_____

_____

_____

_____

_____

_____

Misspelled Words

Read the paragraph from a student's report. Circle the five misspelled words. Then, write the words correctly.

Owls are birds of prey. At night, they come owt of their hiding places. They fly arownd looking for smaller birds. They also look doun on the grownd to find mice. An owl hardly makes any sownd when it hunts.

_____   _____   _____

_____   _____

Lesson 31 Contractions

Say each word. Look at the spelling. Write each word.

Spelling Tip	A contraction is made of two words with one or more letters left out. An apostrophe is a mark that shows where some letters have been left out.

Spelling Words

I'm   _____

can't   _____

you'll   _____

I'll   _____

it's   _____

there's   _____

we'll   _____

don't   _____

that's   _____

wouldn't   _____

Lesson 31 Contractions

Words in Context

Write the contractions that replace the underlined words.

Birthday Party

Dear Josh,

Thank you for inviting me to your party!

(I am) _____ really glad that you

asked me. I know (it is) _____

going to be a lot of fun. I (do not) _____ know if my

sister can come. She'd really like to, but she's got soccer practice

that day. She (can not) _____ miss it or she

(would not) _____ get to play in the next game. If

(there is) _____ any way she can go to your party,

(we will) _____ go together. I've already gotten your

birthday present. (You will) _____ really like it.

(That is) _____ all (I will) _____ say about

it until your party!

Your friend,
Mickey

Lesson 31 Contractions

Fun with Words

Follow the steps to make the spelling word contractions.

1. we will – wi + ' =   _____

2. do not – o + ' =   _____

3. I will – wi + ' =   _____

4. I am – a + ' =   _____

5. can not – no + ' =   _____

6. there is – i + ' =   _____

7. you will – wi + ' =   _____

8. that is – s + ' =   _____

Words Across the Curriculum (Language Arts icon)

Say each contraction. Then, write the contraction.

1. he's   _____   **3.** she's   _____

2. we're   _____   **4.** they're   _____

Write each contraction where it belongs.

My brother is ten years old. _____ older than I am.

My sister is only one. _____ a baby.

_____ both at the park now. When they get home,

_____ all going to have lunch.

Lesson 31 Contractions

Words in Writing

Write a letter to a friend. Use at least three of the words from the box.

I'm	you'll	can't	we'll	that's	he's	she's
it's	I'll	there's	don't	won't	we're	they're

_____

_____

_____

Misspelled Words

Read the letter. Circle the five misspelled contractions. Then, write the words correctly.

Dear Yuri,

   Its' almost summer, and my family will be going to the lake soon. Im' not sure what day wer'e leaving. I think wel'l leave the week after school gets out. I'll let you know as soon as I find out. I cant' wait to see you!

Your friend,
Sam

_____   _____   _____

_____   _____

Lesson 32 Compound Words

Say each word. Listen to the two words that make up the word. Write each word.

Spelling Tip	A compound word is made up of two smaller words.

Spelling Words

into _____

everything _____

sometimes _____

today _____

myself _____

everyone _____

weekend _____

bedroom _____

outside _____

nothing _____

Lesson 32 Compound Words

Words in Context
Write the missing spelling words.

Workday

Challenge

Circle the other compound words in the story.

_____ is Saturday. That means _____ in my family has to do chores. I have to clean my _____ all by _____. I have to make sure that _____ is out of place. Then, I have to wash my clothes and put them _____ my closet. I also have to help my sister clean the bathroom upstairs. After we've done our chores inside the house, we go _____ to work in the yard. _____, we rakes leaves. Other times, we pull the weeds from the flowerbeds. When we've done _____ on our list of chores, we can enjoy the rest of the _____.

Word Building
Combine the words to make compound words.

1. sail + boat = _____

2. birth + day = _____

3. may + be = _____

4. note + book = _____

Lesson 32 Compound Words

Fun with Words

Write the spelling word that includes one of the words from each compound word.

1. cookout _____

5. something _____

2. daytime _____

6. bathroom _____

3. himself _____

7. within _____

4. nowhere _____

8. bookend _____

Words Across the Curriculum

Say each social studies word. Then, write the word.

1. downtown_____

3. classroom _____

2. mailbag _____

4. daylight _____

Write each social studies word next to its definition.

1. a place for students to learn _____

2. a sack to carry letters in _____

3. the time when the sun shines _____

4. the middle of a city _____

Lesson 32 Compound Words

Words in Writing

Write about something your family does on the weekends. Use at least three of the words from the box.

into	sometimes	myself	weekend	outside	downtown	classroom
without	today	everyone	bedroom	nothing	mailbag	daylight

_____

_____

_____

_____

Misspelled Words

Read the description. Circle the five misspelled words. Then, write the words correctly.

Every weekend in the summer, everone in my family comes to my house. My cousins and I play games in my bedrom for a while. Somtimes, we have a cookout outcide in the backyard. The food is always so good that there's nothig left over. I'm sad when everybody has to leave.

_____   _____   _____

_____   _____

Review Lessons 29-32

Write the contraction for each pair of words.

1. you will _____

2. do not _____

3. I am _____

4. there is _____

5. can not _____

6. I will _____

7. we will _____

8. it is _____

9. that is _____

10. will not _____

Write the spelling word that completes each sentence.

1. Please hang your coat on the _____.

2. An _____ sleeps during the day and hunts at night.

3. There is no school on the _____.

4. Some floors are made of _____.

5. I can _____ to 100.

6. On a hot summer day, _____ I go swimming.

Review Lessons 29–32

Write the spelling word that means the opposite.

1. bad   _____

2. in   _____

3. north   _____

4. something   _____

5. gave   _____

6. up   _____

7. empty   _____

8. inside   _____

9. sat   _____

10. quiet   _____

11. no one   _____

12. later   _____

A

an·i·mals *pl. n.* Plural form of *animal*. Any being other than a human being.

a·round *adv.* On all sides.

art *n.* Expression of other objects by painting, drawing, sculpture, etc.

as *adv.* In the same way.

ask *v.* To question.

aunt *n.* A sister of one's father or mother; the wife of one's uncle.

B

ba·by *n.* A young child.

back *n.* The rear part of a structure or object.

bad *adj.* Not good.

band *n.* A group of musicians who join together to play their instruments.

beach·es *pl. n.* Plural of *beach*. Pebbly or sandy shore of a lake, ocean, sea, or river.

be·cause *conj.* For a reason.

bed·room *n.* A room for sleeping.

best *adj.* Better than all others.

bird *n.* A warm-blooded, egg-laying animal, usually able to fly, whose body is covered with feathers.

blank *adj.* Having no markings or writing.

blend *v.* To mix together smoothly.

block *n.* A solid piece of matter. *v.* To stop.

bloom *v.* To bear flowers.

blot *n.* A spot or stain. *v.* To pat dry with a cloth.

books *pl. n.* Plural of *book*. A group of pages fastened together.

both *adj.* Two together.

branch·es *pl. n.* Plural of *branch*. A woody part that grows from the main trunk of a tree.

bread *n.* A food made from flour.

break *v.* To separate into parts.

breeze *n.* A slight, gentle wind.

brick *n.* A molded block.

bright *adj.* Shining color or light.

bring *v.* To carry to a certain place.

brook *n.* A small, freshwater stream.

broom *n.* A long-handled tool used for sweeping.

broth·er *n.* A male who shares the same parents as another person.

brush *n.* A tool with bristles used for applying paint; a tool used to smooth hair *v.* To smooth hair.

bug *n.* Any small insect or life form. *v.* To bother or annoy.

burn *v.* To hurt or destroy by fire.

bush·es *pl. n.* Plural of *bush*. A short, tree-like plant with branches near the ground.

C

came *v.* Past tense of *come*. To travel toward.

camp *n.* A temporary shelter outdoors.

can't *contr.* Short form of *cannot*.

cart *n.* A vehicle for moving items by hand.

carve *v.* To cut into something.

cash *n.* Money.

cast *n.* A covering used on a broken bone. *v.* To throw with force.

catch *v.* To grab from the air.

change *n.* Coins *v.* To make different.

chase *v.* To follow quickly.

chat *v.* To talk in a friendly manner.

chick *n.* A bird that has just hatched.

child *n.* A young person.

cir·cle *n.* A closed curve with all points the same distance from a center point.

clap·ping *v.* Striking the hands together with a loud sound.

class·es *pl. n.* Plural form of *class*. A group of students who study the same subject in the same room.

class·room *n.* A room in a school where students learn.

clean *adj.* Free from dirt. *v.* To remove dirt from an object.

clock *n.* A tool that measures time.

coat *n.* A piece of clothing worn over other clothes to protect a person from weather.

cook *n.* Someone who makes food. *v.* To make food.

cool *adj.* Without warmth.

count *v.* To name numbers in order.

cous·in *n.* A child of one's uncle or aunt.

crowd *n.* A large group of people gathered together.

crown *n.* A head covering worn by royalty.

cry *v.* To shed tears.

cube *n.* A regular solid with six equal sides.

cut·ting *v.* Separating into pieces with a sharp tool.

D

dance *v.* To move the body to music.

dark *adj.* Having little or no light.

day·light *n.* Light during the day.

desk *n.* A table with drawers and a top for writing.

dig·ging *v.* Making a hole in the ground.

dip·ping *v.* Putting something down into a liquid for a moment.

dirt *n.* Soil or earth.

dish *n.* A plate or bowl for food.

dog *n.* A tame member of the wolf family.

don't *contr.* Short form of *do not*.

down *adv.* The direction that is opposite of up.

down·town *adv.* Toward the lower part of a city.

dress *n.* A piece of clothes for girls and women.

drip·ping *v.* Letting a liquid fall in small drops; falling in small drops.

drop *n.* A small amount of a liquid. *v.* To fall or let go of an object in air.

dropped *v.* Past tense of *drop*.

drum *n.* A musical instrument played by beating.

dry *adj.* Free from water or other moisture.

duck *n.* A swimming bird with a short neck and legs. *v.* To lower the head and body quickly.

dump *v.* To drop in one load.

E

each *adj.* Two or more considered separately.

eat *v.* To chew and swallow food.

eight *n.* The number after seven and before nine.

e·qual *adj.* Of the same measurement, quantity, or value as another.

e·ven *adj.* Smooth; able to be divided by two equally.

eve·ry *adj.* All things; all possible.

eve·ry·one *pron.* Everybody; all people.

eye *n.* The organ used to see.

F

fam·i·ly *n.* Parents and their children; a group of people connected by blood or marriage.

far *adv.* At a distance.

farm *n.* Land to grow food or to breed and raise domestic animals.

fast *adj.* Quick.

fa·ther *n.* A male parent.

fifth *adj.* Number five in a series.

find *v.* To discover.

first *adj.* Number one in a series.

fish *n.* A water animal with fins, gills, and usually, scales. *v.* To try to catch fish.

fist *n.* A hand closed tightly.

five *n.* The number after four and before six.

fix *v.* To repair.

flash·es *pl. n.* Plural form of *flash*. Sudden, quick bursts. *v.* Occurs or appears briefly or suddenly.

float *n.* Something that stays on the surface of a liquid. *v.* To stay on the surface of a liquid.

flock *n.* A group of animals of all the same kind, especially birds or sheep.

flow *v.* To move freely.

fog *n.* A mass of condensed water vapor that lies close to the ground.

food *n.* A substance to be eaten.

fort *n.* A building used for defense.

found *v.* Past tense of *find*. Discovered.

four *n.* The number after three and before five.

fox *n.* A wild animal having a pointed snout, upright ears, and a long, bushy tail.

fox·es *pl. n.* Plural form of *fox*.

free *adj.* Able to choose; without cost or payment. *v.* To get loose.

fresh *adj.* Newly made.

friends *pl. n.* Plural form of *friend*. People who are personally liked by another.

frog *n.* A small animal with strong hind legs for hopping.

from *prep.* Starting at a particular time or place.

front *n.* The forward surface of an object or body.

frost *n.* A covering of small ice crystals on a cold surface.

fruit *n.* The part of a plant that has seeds and can be eaten.

G

gar·den *n.* A place for growing flowers, vegetables, or fruit.

girl *n.* A female child or infant.

give *v.* To make a present of.

glad *adj.* A state of being happy.

glass *n.* A clear material used for windows; a clear cup used to hold a drink.

glove *n.* A covering for the hand.

glow *v.* To have a bright, warm color.

glue *n.* Something used to stick and hold items together.

goat *n.* A horned animal related to sheep.

goes *v.* Present tense of *go*. Moves along.

got *v.* Past tense of *get*. Received; gained.

gram *n.* A metric unit of mass and weight.

grand·fa·ther *n.* The father of one's father or mother.

grand·moth·er *n.* The mother of one's father or mother.

grape *n.* A small fruit.

grass *n.* Any of many plants having narrow leaves and jointed stems, usually found on a lawn.

grin *v.* To smile broadly.

grip *n.* A strong hold. *v.* To grab and keep a strong hold on.

ground *n.* The surface of the earth.

grow *v.* To increase in size.

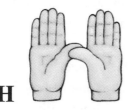

H

ham *n.* Meat that comes from a pig.

hard *adj.* Not soft.

has *v.* Owns.

hat *n.* A covering for the head.

hay *n.* Grass that has been cut and dried for animal food.

he's *contr.* Short form of *he is*.

hear *v.* To listen with the ear.

hid *v.* Past tense of *hide*. Put out of sight.

his *adj.* The possessive form of the pronoun *he*.

hook *n.* A curved object used to hang things. *v.* To catch or grab.

hop *v.* To move with light springing motions.

horse *n.* A large, strong, hoofed animal with a long mane and tail.

hot *adj.* Having heat that is greater than normal body temperature.

hour *n.* A measure of time equal to 60 minutes.

house *n.* A building that serves as living quarters for one or more families.

hugged *v.* Past tense of *hug*. Put one's arms around a person or thing.

hunt *v.* To look for.

hurt *v.* To experience or cause pain.

I

I'll *contr.* Short form of *I will*.

I'm *contr.* Short form of *I am*.

inch *n.* A unit of length. *v.* To move slowly.

in·to *prep.* Inside of.

it's *contr.* Short form of *it is*.

J

jam *n.* A jelly with whole fruit. *v.* To force or wedge into a tight position.

jog *n.* A slow steady run, especially when exercising. *v.* To slowly run.

jump *v.* To spring from the ground into the air.

K

keep *v.* To have and hold on to.

L

lake *n.* A large, inland body of water.

lamp *n.* A device that gives of light.

land *n.* The solid, exposed surface of the earth. *v.* To arrive at a place from water.

last *adj.* Following all the rest. *adv.* After all others.

late *adj.* Happening after the proper or usual time.

leave *v.* To go from.

lend *v.* To give and expect return of something.

length *n.* The distance of something from end to end.

less *adj.* Not as much; fewer.

light *n.* Brightness. *adj.* Having light.

line *n.* A long, thin mark.

list *n.* A series of numbers or words.

lock *n.* A device used to secure or fasten. *v.* To close up securely.

long *adj.* Greater than the normal amount of time or distance.

look *v.* To see. *n.* The act of seeing.

lost *adj.* Unable to find one's way.

lot *n.* A great number or amount; a piece of land having boundaries.

loud *adj.* Having intense sound and high volume.

luck *n.* Good fortune.

lump *n.* A pile. *v.* To group things together.

lunch *n.* The meal between breakfast and dinner.

M

mad *adj.* Angry.

mail·bag *n.* A container for carrying letters.

man *n.* An adult male.

man·y *adj.* Amounting to a large number or amount.

map *n.* A plane surface picture of land.

mark *n.* A dent or stain that can be seen.

mask *n.* A covering used to hide the face.

meet *v.* To come upon face to face.

mess *n.* A disorderly or confused heap.

met *v.* Past tense of *meet*.

me·ter *n.* A metric unit of length.

milk *n.* A white liquid from animals that is a source of food for their young.

mi·nus *prep.* Reduced by subtraction.

mist *n.* A cloud of water droplets in the air.

mix *v.* To blend into one.

mon·ey *n.* Anything that has value and is used in exchange.

month *n.* One of the twelve divisions of a calendar year.

moon *n.* Earth's natural satellite.

more *adj.* Greater number, size, or degree.

moth·er *n.* A female parent.

mouse *n.* A small rodent.

must *v.* To have to.

my·self *pron.* The one who is me.

N

new *adj.* Not used before.

next *adj.* Immediately following.

nice *adj.* Pleasing.

night *n.* The hours of darkness.

nine *n.* The number after eight and before ten.

ninth *adj.* Number nine in a series.

north *n.* The direction to a person's left while facing east.

nose *n.* The facial feature containing the nostrils, used to smell.

noth•ing *n.* Not anything.

now *adv.* At this time.

num•ber *n.* A word or symbol that is used in counting.

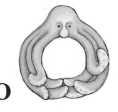

O

off *adv.* No longer on or connected. *prep.* Away from.

once *adv.* A single time.

one *adj.* Single. *n.* A single person.

our *adj.* Of or relating to us. *pron.* The possessive case of the pronoun *we*.

out *adv.* Away from the inside. *adj.* Away. *prep.* Through.

out•side *n.* The area not inside.

owl *n.* A bird that is active at night.

own *adj.* Belonging to oneself. *v.* To possess.

P

pack *n.* A group of things tied or wrapped up. *v.* To put things together.

pan *n.* A container used for cooking.

par•ent *n.* A mother or father.

park *n.* Land used for playing or relaxing. *v.* To leave something in a parking garage or lot, as a car.

part *n.* A segment, portion, or division of a whole. *v.* To leave or go away from.

past *adj.* Having to do with or existing at an earlier time. *n.* Before the present time. *adv.* To go by. *prep.* After.

paste *n.* A mixture used to stick things together.

pat *v.* To tap lightly with a hand.

path *n.* A track or trail.

peck *v.* To strike with a beak.

pen *n.* A writing tool that uses ink.

pen•cil *n.* A writing or drawing tool whose marks can be erased.

peo•ple *n.* Human beings.

pick *v.* To choose from a group; to take off a tree.

pin *n.* A piece of wire used to hold something together.

pine *n.* A cone-bearing evergreen tree.

pint *n.* A liquid or dry measurement equal to half a quart.

pit *n.* The hard stone of a fruit.

place *n.* An area.

plan *n.* A way to do something.

plant *n.* A living organism belonging to the vegetable kingdom. *v.* To place a living organism in the ground for growing.

play *v.* To amuse or entertain oneself.

please *v.* To be so kind as to make happy; used to ask politely.

plot *n.* A small piece of ground; the main story line.

plum *n.* A small fruit.

plus *prep.* Added to.

pond *n.* A small body of still water, smaller than a lake.

pool *n.* A small body of water, often made by human beings for swimming.

pose *v.* To place.

pull *n.* The act of moving something toward the force. *v.* To cause motion in the same direction of.

push *n.* The act of moving something away from the force. *v.* To move forward by force.

R

race *n.* A contest judged by speed.

rain *n.* Water that falls to Earth in the form of drops.

ramp *n.* A slope that connects two different levels.

reach *v.* To stretch out; to touch or grasp; to arrive at a place.

read *v.* To look at and understand the meaning of something written.

right *adj.* Correct. *n.* The direction opposite left.

ring *n.* A circular mark, line, or object; a small, circular band worn on a finger.

rip *v.* To tear apart.

road *n.* A highway used for cars and trucks.

rob•in *n.* A bird with a black head and reddish breast.

rock *n.* A hard naturally formed material.

room *n.* An area of a building set off by walls.

rose *n.* A plant that has flowers and prickly stems.

row *n.* A group of things next to each other in line. *v.* To move a boat with oars.

rude *adj.* Not polite.

rug *n.* A cloth used to cover a floor.

run•ning *v.* Moving quickly.

S

sack *n.* A strong bag.

safe *adj.* Not in danger. *n.* A strong metal container used to protect items.

sail *n.* A fabric used to catch wind and cause a ship to move. *v.* To move over water in a boat.

sand *n.* Fine grains of rock found in deserts and on beaches.

sea *n.* The body of salt water that covers most of Earth.

sec•ond *n.* A very short period of time. *adj.* Next after the first.

send *v.* To cause something to be moved from one place to another.

set *n.* A group. *v.* To put or place.

sev•en *n.* The number after six and before eight.

shack *n.* A small, roughly built hut or cabin.

shade *n.* A place sheltered from the rays of the sun.

shad•ow *n.* A dark shape cast by a person or thing as it blocks the sun's light.

shake *v.* To move back and forth quickly.

shall *v.* Will.

share *v.* To use together.

sharp *adj.* Having a fine point that can cut.

she's *contr.* Short form of *she is*.

shine *v.* To give off light.

shoe *n.* An outer covering for a foot.

shore *n.* The land next to a body of water.

short *adj.* Having little height or length.

signs *pl. n.* Plural form of *sign*. Objects with information written on them. *v.* To write one's name on.

sis•ter *n.* A female having the same parents as another.

sit *v.* To rest the body on a seat.

six *n.* The number after five and before seven.

skip•ped *v.* Past tense of skip. Moved in light jumps or leaps.

slam *v.* To shut with force.

slant *v.* To be in a sloped position.

sled *n.* A vehicle used to travel on snow or ice.

sleep *n.* A natural state of rest. *v.* To rest while not awake.

slice *n.* A thinly cut piece. *v.* To cut into slices.

slide *v.* To move smoothly across a surface.

slip *v.* To fall or lose one's balance.

slipped *v.* Past tense of *slip*.

slit *n.* A thin opening. *v.* To cut a thin opening into something.

slow *adj.* Moving at a low rate of speed; not fast.

snack *n.* A small amount of food eaten between meals.

soap *n.* A substance used for washing.

soft *adj.* Feeling smooth to the touch; not stiff or hard.

some•times *adv.* Not always.

song *n.* A piece of poetry set to music.

soon *adv.* In a short time.

sound *n.* A noise heard by the ears.

south *n.* The direction opposite of north.

space *n.* An area; the area beyond Earth's atmosphere.

speak *v.* To say words.

speech•es *pl. n.* Plural form of *speech*. A talk given to a group of people.

spend *v.* To pay or use money.

spi•der *n.* An eight-legged bug that spins a web.

spill *v.* To cause something to flow or fall out of a container.

spin *v.* To turn something around and around.

spoon *n.* A smooth, curved eating or cooking tool.

sport *n.* A game or physical activity with set rules.

spot *n.* A small mark that is different from the area around it.

spray *n.* A liquid moved in a fine mist or droplets. *v.* To force small drops of a liquid through air.

spy *n.* One who watches other people secretly.

stack *n.* A large pile. *v.* To put things in a pile.

stand *v.* To move to an upright position. *n.* A device on which something rests.

start *v.* To begin. *n.* The beginning of something.

states *pl. n.* Plural form of *state*. One of an area of a land. *v.* To make known verbally.

stay *v.* To remain. *n.* A short visit.

stepped *v.* Past tense of *step*. To move by lifting and putting one's foot down.

stick *n.* A thin piece of wood.

sting *v.* To poke with something sharp.

store *n.* A business that has items for sale. *v.* To put something away for a long time.

stuck *v.* Held or trapped in one place.

stu•dents *pl. n.* Plural form of *student*. Learners.

sub•tract *v.* To take away from.

such *adj.* Of an extreme degree or amount.

sum *n.* The result of adding.

T

tack *n.* A short nail with a flat head.

take *v.* To get hold of.

tapped *v.* Past tense of *tap*. Hit lightly.

taste *v.* To notice the flavor of something.

teach *v.* To pass on knowledge; to give lessons.

team *n.* Two or more players on one side in a game.

teeth *pl. n.* The plural form of *tooth*. Hard objects in the mouth used for chewing.

tell *v.* To say or describe.

ten *n.* The number after nine and before eleven.

test *n.* An exam; a way to find out what someone knows or has learned.

that's *contr.* Short form of *that is*.

them *pron.* Those people or things.

there's *contr.* Short form of *there is*.

they're *contr.* Short from of they are.

thing *n.* An object.

think *v.* To use one's mind.

third *adj.* Coming next after second.

those *adj.* The ones over there.

three *n.* The number after two and before four.

toad *n.* A small animal like a frog that lives on dry land.

to·day *adv.* On or during the present day. *n.* The present day.

to·geth·er *adv.* In one pair or group.

too *adv.* Also.

town *n.* A group of buildings smaller than a city.

trail *n.* A path through woods.

trap *n.* A device for catching animals. *v.* To catch by surprise.

tree *n.* A tall, woody plant.

trick *n.* An action meant to fool.

trip *n.* A visit from one place to another. *v.* To stumble.

try *v.* To make an attempt.

tube *n.* A hollow cylinder.

tug *v.* To pull with force.

tune *n.* A simple song.

turn *v.* To rotate.

tur·tle *n.* An animal covered with a hard shell.

two *n.* The number after one and before three.

U

un·cle *n.* The brother of one's mother or father; the husband of an aunt.

us *pron.* You and me.

use *v.* To put to work.

V

ver·y *adv.* To a high or great degree.

W

wait *v.* To stay in one place until something happens.

watch·es *n.* Plural of *watch*. Small clocks worn on

people's wrists. *v.* Looks at with attention.

we'll *contr.* Short form of *we will.*

we're *contr.* Short form of *we are.*

week *n.* A period of seven days.

week·end *n.* The end of the week from the period of Friday evening through Sunday evening.

went *v.* Past tense of *go.* Moved away from; left.

were *v.* Plural past tense of *to be.* Existed.

wheat *n.* A grain used to make breads and similar foods.

wheel *n.* A round disk that turns on an axle.

where *adv.* At or in what direction or place.

which *pron.* What one or ones.

while *n.* A length or period of time.

whip *v.* To hit or beat many times.

why *adj.* For what reason or purpose.

wide *adj.* Covering a large area.

width *n.* The distance of something from side to side.

will *v.* To be about to or going to.

wind *n.* A natural movement of air.

wing *n.* One of the movable structures that allow a bird or insect to fly; one of the airfoils on either side of an aircraft.

win·ning *adj.* Succeeding over others.

wish *v.* To want something.

with *prep.* Alongside of; in possession of something.

with·out *adv.* On the outside; not in possession of. *prep.* Something or someone lacking.

woke *v.* Past tense of *wake.* To stop sleeping.

wool *n.* The soft, thick hair of sheep and other such mammals; a fabric made from that hair.

wouldn't *contr.* Short form of *would not.*

Y

yard *n.* The ground around or near a house or building.

yet *adv.* Up to now.

you'll *contr.* Short form of *you will.*

Z

zip *v.* To open or close with a zipper; to move with speed.

zoo *n.* A public display or collection of living animals.

Parts of Speech

adj. = adjective

adv. = adverb

art. = article

conj. = conjunction

n. = noun

prep. = preposition

pron. = pronoun

v. = verb

Answer Key

Say each word. Listen to the short **a** sound. Write the word.

Spelling Tip	The short **a** sound is often spelled **a**. The sign for short **a** is /a/.

Spelling Words

has	has
man	man
ham	ham
hat	hat
pan	pan
mad	mad
as	as
jam	jam
bad	bad
pat	pat

6

Words in Context

Write the missing spelling words to finish the rhyme.

My Dad and His Cat

Challenge
Circle the other words in the rhyme with the short **a** sound.

My dad is a _____ man _____ .

He _____ has _____ a pet cat.

The cat's name is Nan.

She likes to chase rats.

My dad's really _____ mad _____ .

Nan chewed up his _____ hat _____ .

That cat is so _____ bad _____ ,

I won't give her a _____ pat _____ .

_____ As _____ soon as he can,

Dad will make bread and _____ jam _____ .

He will get out a _____ pan _____ ,

And then cook some _____ ham _____ .

7

Fun with Words

Write the spelling word that goes with each word.

1. eggs	ham	4. bread	jam
2. pot	pan	5. woman	man
3. coat	hat	6. pet	pat

Write the spelling word that means the opposite of each word.

1. good _____ bad _____
2. glad _____ mad _____

Words Across the Curriculum

Say each social studies word. Then, write each word.

1. map	map	3. cash	cash
2. path	path	4. chat	chat

Write each social studies word where it belongs.

1. We will walk on the garden _____ path _____ .
2. Coins and dollars are _____ cash _____ .
3. A _____ map _____ shows the state you live in.
4. Do you like to _____ chat _____ with friends?

8

Words in Writing

Do you have to do chores at home? Write a list of chores that must be done at home. Use at least three words from the box.

has	ham	pan	as	bad	map	cash
man	hat	mad	jam	pat	path	chat

Answers will vary.

Misspelled Words

Read the student's list of things to do after school. Circle the five misspelled words. Then, write the words correctly on the lines.

1. Put away my coat and het. _____ hat _____
2. Make a snack of bread and jem. _____ jam _____
3. Clean every pot and pen in the sink. _____ pan _____
4. Pate my cat as soon as I find her. _____ Pat _____
5. Walk my dog on the peth in the park. _____ path _____

9

Answer Key

Page 10

Say each word. Listen to the short **i** sound. Write the word.

Spelling Tip	The short **i** sound is often spelled **i**. The sign for short **i** is /i/.

Spelling Words

pin	pin
sit	sit
fix	fix
will	will
zip	zip
dish	dish
his	his
rip	rip
hid	hid
wish	wish

10

Page 11

Words in Context
Write the missing spelling words.

Challenge
Circle the other words in the paragraph with the short **i** sound.

A Bad Day

Today has been a bad day. I ___will___ be glad when (it's) over. As I made lunch, I broke a ___dish___. Just as I was about to ___sit___ down and eat, I stepped on a tack. After lunch, I tried to (give) my cat a bath. He ran outside and ___hid___ from me because he doesn't like to get ___his___ fur wet. As I started to ___zip___ up my coat, I saw a (big) ___rip___ (in) (it) I had to ___fix___ (it) (with) a ___pin___. I ___wish___ (this) day would end soon!

Word Building
Add **p**, **g**, **t**, or **ll** to make new words.

1. si ___sip or sill___
2. wi ___wig or will___
3. hi ___hit, hip, or hill___
4. ti ___tip or till___
5. di ___dip, dig, or dill___
6. fi ___fill, fit, or fig___
7. ji ___jig___
8. bi ___big, bit, or bill___

11

Page 12

Fun with Words
Unscramble the letters to make the spelling words.

1. dhi ___hid___
2. pri ___rip___
3. xif ___fix___
4. nip ___pin___
5. swih ___wish___
6. ist ___sit___
7. lilw ___will___
8. pzi ___zip___
9. sdhi ___dish___
10. shi ___his___

Words Across the Curriculum
Say each science word. Then, write each word.

1. fish ___fish___
2. milk ___milk___
3. mix ___mix___
4. pit ___pit___

Write each science word next to its definition.

1. to blend together ___mix___
2. a drink that comes from cows ___milk___
3. a water animal with fins ___fish___
4. the seed in a plum ___pit___

12

Page 13

Words in Writing
Make up a silly rhyme. Use at least three words from the box.

pin	fix	zip	his	hid	fish	milk
sit	will	dish	rip	wish	mix	pit

Answers will vary.

Misspelled Words
Read the rhyme. Circle the four misspelled words. Then, write the words correctly on the lines.

1. Tim had a (wiss.) ___wish___
2. He wished for a (fesh.) ___fish___
3. When he looked at (hes) (dishe) ___his___ ___dish___
4. One appeared with a swish!

13

Answer Key

Say each word. Listen to the middle sound. Write the word.

Spelling Tip	The short **o** sound and the /ô/ sound are often spelled **o**. The sign for short **o** is /o/. /o/ sound: h**o**p /ô/ sound: d**o**g

Spelling Words

hop	hop
lot	lot
jog	jog
got	got
dog	dog
spot	spot
off	off
lost	lost
soft	soft
long	long

14

Words in Context
Write the missing spelling words.

> **Challenge**
> Circle the other words in the story with the short **o** or /ô/ sounds.

My Lost Dog

When I _____ got _____ up today, I could not find my _____ dog _____ Molly. She was _____ lost _____! I took a _____ jog _____ around the block to look for her. After a _____ long _____ time, I saw Molly. Her collar was coming _____ off _____ her neck. She had a _____ lot _____ of mud all over her legs. One foot was hurt. Molly had to _____ hop _____ on three legs. I patted her _____ soft _____ fur and rubbed the hurt _____ spot _____ on her foot.

Word Building
Add **s** to tell what a girl is doing. Then, write the word.

1. I jog. She jog__s__.   jogs
2. I hop. She hop__s__.   hops
3. I mop. She mop__s__.   mops
4. I chop. She chop__s__.   chops
5. I shop. She shop__s__.   shops

15

Fun with Words
Write the spelling word that means the opposite.

1. on	off	3. short	long
2. hard	soft	4. found	lost

Write the spelling word or words that rhyme with each word.

1. top	hop	
2. hog	jog	dog
3. not	spot	got
	lot	

Words Across the Curriculum
Say each science word. Then, write each word.

1. fox	fox	3. fog	fog
2. hot	hot	4. robin	robin

Write the science word that belongs with each pair of words.

1. rain, dew   fog
2. bluebird, crow   robin
3. warm, burning,   hot
4. dog, wolf   fox

16

Words in Writing
Have you ever lost a pet? Make a poster that tells about a lost pet. Use at least three words from the box.

Answers will vary.

hop	jog	dog	off	soft	fox	fog
lot	got	spot	lost	long	hot	robin

Dictionary Practice
Words in the dictionary are in ABC order. Write the word from the box that comes between each pair of words.

1. pan	robin	soft
2. hug	jog	lap
3. fox	got	hat
4. long	lost	lot
5. mop	off	pit

17

Spectrum Spelling
Grade 2

Answer Key

163

Answer Key

Say each word. Listen to the ending sound. Write the word.

Spelling Tip	The /k/ sound at the end of a word is often spelled **ck**.

Spelling Words

sack	sack
pack	pack
rock	rock
back	back
chick	chick
pick	pick
stick	stick
flock	flock
snack	snack
peck	peck

18

Words in Context
Write the missing spelling words.

Challenge
Circle the other words in the journal entry with the /k/ sound.

At the Farm

Today, I went to _____ **pick** _____ apples from trees on a farm. I had to _____ **pack** _____ them all in a big _____ **sack** _____. Then, I sat on a _____ **rock** _____. I ate a (stack) of (crackers) for a _____ **snack** _____. A _____ **flock** _____ of (black) birds landed near me. One little bird was only a _____ **chick** _____. It turned its (neck) and saw a brown _____ **stick** _____ on the ground. The baby bird began to _____ **peck** _____ at it with its (beak). Then, it ran _____ **back** _____ to its mother.

Word Building
Add **s** to each word to make words that tell about more than one.

1. one pack, two _____ **packs** _____
2. one chick, two _____ **chicks** _____
3. one rock, two _____ **rocks** _____
4. one flock, two _____ **flocks** _____
5. one snack, two _____ **snacks** _____

19

Fun with Words
Each word below has at least one spelling word in it. Circle each spelling word that you find.

1. (chick)en
2. (pick)ing
3. (pack)er
4. (snack)ing
5. (stick)
6. (back)(pack)
7. (rock)y
8. (flock)ed
9. (rock)er
10. (peck)ing

Words Across the Curriculum
Say each social studies word. Then, write each word.

1. lock _____ **lock** _____
2. shack _____ **shack** _____
3. clock _____ **clock** _____
4. tack _____ **tack** _____

Write each social studies word next to the pair of words it belongs with.

1. time, watch _____ **clock** _____
2. pin, nail _____ **tack** _____
3. shut, bolt _____ **lock** _____
4. home, hut _____ **shack** _____

20

Words in Writing
Write about some things you might see and do on a farm. Use at least three words from the box.

sack	rock	chick	stick	snack	lock	clock
pack	back	pick	flock	peck	shack	tack

Answers will vary.

Misspelled Words
Read the student's list of jobs she does on her farm. Circle the five misspelled words. Then, write the words correctly on the lines.

1. Feed the (fleck) of ducks and the (chiks).
   - _____ **flock** _____
   - _____ **chicks** _____
2. Pick up the (stecks) and (rocs) in the yard.
   - _____ **sticks** _____
   - _____ **rocks** _____
3. (Pak) the eggs in a box.
   - _____ **Pack** _____

21

Spectrum Spelling
Grade 2

164

Answer Key

Answer Key

Page 22

Say each word. Listen to the **nd** and **st** sounds. Write the word.

Spelling Tip	The **nd** and **st** sounds are spelled **nd** and **st**.

Spelling Words

fast	fast
list	list
band	band
past	past
fist	fist
pond	pond
last	last
stand	stand
cast	cast
stack	stack

22

Page 23

Words in Context
Write the missing spelling words.

A Day at the Fair

<table><tr><td>Challenge</td></tr><tr><td>Circle the other words in the journal entry with **nd** or **st**.</td></tr></table>

_____Last_____ week, I went to the fair. I

heard a _____band_____ play music. Then, I went

to a food _____stand_____. It had a sign with a

_____list_____ of good things to eat. I decided to

have a _____stack_____ of pancakes (and) some

milk. I couldn't eat very _____fast_____ because I

had a _____cast_____ on my broken (hand.) I couldn't make a

_____fist_____ to hold my fork. After I ate, (just) watched some

ducks as I walked _____past_____ the _____pond_____.

Word Building
Add **nd** or **st** to make new words. Then, write the words.

1. ki **nd** _____kind_____
2. **st** ir _____stir_____
3. **st** amp _____stamp_____
4. se **nd** _____send_____

23

Page 24

Fun with Words
Use the clues to solve the puzzle with spelling words.

Down
1. opposite of slow
3. a small lake
4. a pile
6. a note of things to do

Across
2. opposite of sit
3. by
5. a wrap for a broken bone
6. opposite of first

Words Across the Curriculum
Say each science word. Then, write each word.

1. sand _____sand_____   3. land _____land_____
2. wind _____wind_____   4. mist _____mist_____

Write the missing science words.

1. Fog is a _____mist_____ of tiny water drops.
2. Earth has oceans and _____land_____.
3. _____Wind_____ is moving air.
4. Beaches have _____sand_____ instead of dirt.

24

Page 25

Words in Writing
Why do people like to go camping?
Write an ad that tells why a campsite is
fun. Use at least three words from the box.

fast	band	fist	last	cast	sand	land
list	past	pond	stand	stack	wind	mist

Answers will vary.

Misspelled Words
Read the student's ad for a campsite. Circle the six misspelled words.
Then, write the words on the lines below.

This is your last chance to get a good campsite! We have a (pon)
where you can go fishing. You can fish from a boat or from the (lande.) If
the (wid) and (miste) make you cold, you can make a campfire. There is a
(stak) of wood that you can use. Call us soon. These campsites will go (fasst!)

pond	wind	stack
land	mist	fast

25

Answer Key

Write the five spelling words that rhyme with **tack**.

1. pack
2. sack
3. back
4. snack
5. stack

Write the spelling word that means the opposite of each word.

1. first — last
2. on — off
3. happy — mad
4. break — fix
5. sit — stand
6. found — lost
7. slow — fast
8. won't — will
9. good — bad
10. short — long

26

Write the spelling word that belongs with each pair of words.

1. want, hope — wish
2. walk, run — jog
3. mine, hers — his
4. plate, bowl — dish
5. stone, pebble — rock
6. tear, cut — rip
7. pot, kettle — pan
8. boy, woman — man

Write the spelling word that fits in each sentence.

1. A __flock__ of birds landed near me.
2. The cat has __soft__, fluffy fur.
3. I will __pick__ flowers for my mom.
4. The fish swam in the __pond__.
5. My dad made a __list__ of jobs for me to do.
6. I like __jam__ on my toast.
7. My dog has a white __spot__ on his face.
8. I will __zip__ up my coat.

27

Say each word. Listen for the short **u** sound. Write the word.

Spelling Tip	The short **u** sound is often spelled **u**. The sign for short **u** is /u/.

Spelling Words

us	us
rug	rug
luck	luck
tug	tug
must	must
hunt	hunt
bug	bug
duck	duck
stuck	stuck
lunch	lunch

28

Words in Context

Write the missing spelling words.

Good Luck for a Bug

Challenge

Circle the other words in the journal entry with the short **u** sound.

My friend Russ and I went to the park. We stopped near the pond to eat our __lunch__. We spread a blanket like a __rug__ on the grass. We had to __tug__ on the ends to smooth out the blanket. As we ate, we saw a __duck__ swim toward __us__. Then, it started to __hunt__ for something to eat. The duck saw a small water __bug__. The duck rushed toward the bug, but it got __stuck__ in some mud. The bug swam away. It __must__ have had really good __luck__!

Word Building

Add **s** to each word to make words that tell about more than one.

1. one bug, two __bugs__
2. one duck, two __ducks__
3. one hut, two __huts__
4. one tub, two __tubs__
5. one hug, two __hugs__

29

Spectrum Spelling
Grade 2

Answer Key

Answer Key

Fun with Words

Change the vowel in each word to make a spelling word.

1. mist   must
2. is   us
3. rag   rug
4. hint   hunt
5. lick   luck
6. tag   tug
7. big   bug
8. stack   stuck

Words Across the Curriculum

Say each math word. Then, write each word.

1. sum   sum   3. number   number
2. plus   plus   4. subtract   subtract

Write the missing math words.

When you add one   number   to another, you find the   sum   . You use a   plus   sign to show that you are adding. You use a minus sign when you   subtract   .

30

Words in Writing

Write about a good day you had. Use at least three words from the box.

| us | luck | must | bug | stuck | sum | number |
| rug | tug | hunt | duck | lunch | plus | subtract |

Answers will vary.

Dictionary Practice

Write each word from the box in ABC order.

BCDEFGHI	JKLMNOPQ	RSTUVWXYZ
bug	luck	rug
duck	lunch	stuck
hunt	must	subtract
	number	sum
	plus	tug
		us

31

Say each word. Listen for the short **e** sound. Write the word.

Spelling Tip — The short **e** sound is often spelled **e**. The sign for short **e** is /e/.

Spelling Words

pen	pen
met	met
rest	rest
send	send
yet	yet
tell	tell
them	them
went	went
best	best
mess	mess

32

Words in Context

Write the missing spelling words.

Challenge

Circle the other words in the letter with the short **e** sound.

At the Pet Shop

Dear Meg,

I have to   tell   you about my trip to the pet shop. I   went   there yesterday and   met   my friend Rick. We saw some pups playing in a   pen   . After a while, they sat down to   rest   . They were so cute that I wanted to take all of   them   home. I called Mom to see if I could get one pup. I promised not to let it make a   mess   in the house. I told Mom it would be the   best   birthday present she could get me. She said yes! I haven't named my new pup   yet   .   Send   me a letter soon!

Love,
Ben

33

Answer Key

Answer Key

Fun with Words

Add and subtract the letters to make spelling words.

1. chin – ch + gr = **grin**

2. mess – m + dr = **dress**

3. ripe + t – e = **trip**

4. plum – pl + dr = **drum**

5. chick – ch + tr = **trick**

6. rope + d – e = **drop**

7. map – m + tr = **trap**

8. chip – ch + gr = **grip**

Words Across the Curriculum

Say each science word. Then, write each word.

1. tree **tree**   3. grass **grass**

2. grow **grow**   4. gram **gram**

Write the missing science words.

A **tree** is a tall plant with a trunk and leaves. One big leaf might weigh about one **gram**.

Grass is a short plant that can **grow** very fast.

38

Words in Writing

Write a funny story about a trick that a pet can do. Use at least three words from the box.

_____

_____

_____   Answers will vary.

_____

drop	dry	drum	grip	try	tree	grass
trap	grin	trip	trick	dress	grow	gram

Dictionary Practice

A dictionary has symbols that tell how to say words. Write the word or words from the box that have the sound of each short-vowel symbol.

/a/ **grass**   **gram**   **trap**

/e/ **dress**

/i/ **grin**   **grip**   **trip**

trick

/o/ **grow**

/u/ **drum**

39

Say each word. Listen to the beginning sound. Write the word.

Spelling Tip	The **bl**, **gl**, and **pl** sounds are spelled the way they sound.

Spelling Words

plum **plum**

glass **glass**

bloom **bloom**

glow **glow**

glad **glad**

plan **plan**

block **block**

plot **plot**

glove **glove**

plant **plant**

40

Words in Context

Write the missing spelling words.

An Indoor Garden

Challenge
Circle the other words in the story with **bl**, **gl**, or **pl**.

I drew a **plan** for an indoor garden. It will be in a room with (plenty) of windows made of **glass**. The windows won't **block** the **glow** of the sun. First, I will **plant** a **plum** tree. I'll wear a **glove** on one hand when (place) the tree in the rich (black) dirt. My garden will also have a **plot** for flowers. Everyone will be **glad** when they **bloom**.

Word Building

Add **es** to make words that mean more than one. Then, write the new words.

1. one glass, two glass **es**   **glasses**

2. one dress, two dress **es**   **dresses**

3. one fox, two fox **es**   **foxes**

4. one class, two class **es**   **classes**

5. one lunch, two lunch **es**   **lunches**

6. one bunch, two bunch **es**   **bunches**

41

Spectrum Spelling
Grade 2

Answer Key

Fun with Words
Circle the hidden spelling words.

```
p  l  g (b  l  o  c  k) g
n (g  l  a  s  s) g  r  l
(p  l  o  t  g (p  l  a  n
 l  a  w  c  l  p  o  d  e
 a  s  l  n  a  l  v  g  d
 n  w  u  t  d  u  e  l  t
 t (b  l  o  o  m) o  l  s
```

Words Across the Curriculum
Say each art word. Then, write each word.

I. blot ___blot___   3. blank ___blank___

2. blend ___blend___

Write the art words where they belong.

You can create a colorful picture on a ___blank___ sheet
of paper. You can ___blend___ different colors of paint
together. You can use a cloth to ___blot___ the paint dry.

42

Words in Writing
Write a description of an artwork you made.
Use at least three of the words from the box.

_____

_____

_____   Answers will vary.

_____

| plum | bloom | glad | block | glove | blot | blend |
| glass | glow | plan | plot | plant | glue | blank |

Dictionary Practice
Some words have more than one meaning. A dictionary tells all the
meanings of words. Write the word from the box next to its two meanings.

I. the action in a story; a small piece of ground ___plot___

2. a square piece of wood; to be in the way ___block___

3. a living thing that has leaves; to put in the ground ___plant___

4. something to drink from; what a window is made of ___glass___

43

Say each word. Listen to the ending sound. Write the word.

| Spelling Tip | The /mp/, /ng/, and /sk/ sounds are spelled **ng**, **mp**, and **sk** |

Spelling Words

ask	___ask___
camp	___camp___
wing	___wing___
desk	___desk___
sting	___sting___
jump	___jump___
lamp	___lamp___
bring	___bring___
dump	___dump___
ramp	___ramp___

44

Words in Context
Write the missing spelling words.

Fun Away from Home

| Challenge |
| Circle the other words in the story with **ng**, **mp**, or **sk**. |

Dear Carlos,

I'm having a great time at ___camp___! In the morning,
we run down a long ___ramp___ and ___jump___
into the lake. Then, we each have to do a task. I have to
___bring___ the trash outside. Then, I ___dump___ it
in a large bin. Once, there was a pesky bee with a black spot on one
___wing___ near the bin. I was afraid it might
___sting___ me, but it flew away. At night, we sing songs or
perform funny skits, sit at the ___desk___ in my room. I turn
on the ___lamp___ and read a book. You should
___ask___ your mom if you
can come to camp next year.

Your friend,
Mike

45

Answer Key

Fun with Words

Write the spelling word that fits each tongue-twister.

1. Can Carlos come to _____ **camp** ?

2. Don't _____ **dump** _____ dirt down the drain.

3. Ron ran in the rain on the _____ **ramp** _____.

4. _____ **Bring** _____ Brad the broken brown branch.

5. Jack will just _____ **jump** _____ over Jim's jeep.

6. Lily looked at the light leaving the _____ **lamp** _____.

7. _____ **Ask** _____ Ann to add all the apples.

8. One _____ **wing** _____ of the wasp was white.

Words Across the Curriculum

Say each art word. Then, write each word.

1. song _____ **song** _____   3. ring _____ **ring** _____

2. mask _____ **mask** _____   4. lump _____ **lump** _____

Write each art word next to the correct clue.

1. This could be a piece of clay. _____ **lump** _____

2. You can sing this. _____ **song** _____

3. This hides your face. _____ **mask** _____

4. A bell makes this sound. _____ **ring** _____

46

Words in Writing

Write some questions that you would ask a camp worker about a camp you might like to visit. Use at least three words from the box.

ask	wing	sting	lamp	dump	song	ring
camp	desk	jump	bring	ramp	mask	lump

_____

_____ *Answers will vary.*

_____

Misspelled Words

Read the student's questions. Circle the six misspelled words. Then, write the words correctly.

1. Are there any bugs that can (stinge)?   _____ **sting** _____

2. Should (breng) my own (lammp)?   _____ **bring** _____

   _____ **lamp** _____

3. Do you have a (desck) that I can use?   _____ **desk** _____

4. Do we have to (aks) before we (jemp)   _____ **ask** _____

   in the lake?   _____ **jump** _____

47

Write the spelling word that belongs with each pair of words.

1. hat, scarf, _____ **glove** _____

2. guitar, trumpet, _____ **drum** _____

3. apple, peach, _____ **plum** _____

4. hop, skip, _____ **jump** _____

5. smile, laugh, _____ **grin** _____

6. shirt, pants, _____ **dress** _____

Write the spelling word that rhymes with each pair of words.

1. bent, sent, _____ **went** _____

2. rust, just, _____ **must** _____

3. mad, sad, _____ **glad** _____

4. lip, drip, _____ **trip** _____

5. nest, pest, _____ **best** _____

6. blot, slot, _____ **plot** _____

7. bunch, crunch, _____ **lunch** _____

8. sell, bell, _____ **tell** _____

48

Some of the spelling words are action words. Write each spelling word next to its meaning.

1. to pull on _____ **tug** _____

2. to fall _____ **drop** _____

3. to hold on to _____ **grip** _____

4. to think ahead _____ **plan** _____

5. to capture _____ **trap** _____

6. to question _____ **ask** _____

Write the missing spelling words.

1. Did you _____ **bring** _____ your books home?

2. I will _____ **send** _____ you a letter soon.

3. The truck is _____ **stuck** _____ in the mud.

4. Which song do you think is the _____ **best** _____?

5. I poured some milk in my _____ **glass** _____.

6. Li will _____ **try** _____ to win the race.

7. The roses will _____ **bloom** _____ in the spring.

8. Turn on the _____ **lamp** _____ so you can see.

49

Answer Key

Say each word. Listen for the long **a** sound. Write the word.

Spelling Tip	The long **a** sound can be spelled **a-consonant-e**, **ay**, and **ai**. The sign for the long **a** sound is /ā/.

Spelling Words

lake	lake
stay	stay
wait	wait
take	take
play	play
came	came
rain	rain
safe	safe
late	late
sail	sail

50

Words in Context
Write the missing spelling words.

A Rainy Day

Challenge
Circle the other words in the story with the /ā/ sound.

I did not want to _____ stay _____ in (today.) I was ready to _____ play _____ outside. But it was too _____ late _____! The sky was (gray) and _____ rain _____ was falling. I went inside to (make) sure I was _____ safe _____ from the storm. I didn't have to _____ wait _____ very long before the sun _____ came _____ out. I decided to _____ take _____ my toy boat outside. I (placed) it in a puddle so it could _____ sail _____ like a ship in a _____ lake _____.

Word Building
Add **ing** to tell what the boys are doing. Then, write the words.

1. The boys play. The boys are play___ing___.   playing
2. The boys sail. The boys are sail___ing___.   sailing
3. The boys stay. The boys are stay___ing___.   staying
4. The boys wait. The boys are wait___ing___.   waiting

51

Fun with Words
Write the missing letters to make the /ā/ sound in the spelling words.

1. s_a_f_e_
2. c_a_m_e_
3. w_a_i_t
4. st_a_y_
5. l_a_t_e_
6. r_a_i_n
7. t_a_k_e_
8. pl_a_y_
9. s_a_i_l
10. l_a_k_e_

Words Across the Curriculum
Say each science word. Then, write each word.

1. hay _____ hay _____
2. taste _____ taste _____
3. trail _____ trail _____
4. grape _____ grape _____

Write each science word next to its definition.

1. to sense the flavor of _____ taste _____
2. a path in the woods _____ trail _____
3. food for a horse _____ hay _____
4. a fruit that grows on a vine _____ grape _____

52

Words in Writing
Imagine that you are at bat in a baseball game. Write a description of what happens. Use at least three words from the box.

lake	wait	play	rain	late	hay	trail
stay	take	came	safe	sail	bait	grape

Answers will vary.

Misspelled Words
Read the student's description of part of a baseball game. Circle the six misspelled words. Then, write the words correctly.

I (caim) up to the plate. The pitcher did not (tayke) long to throw a fast ball. I swung my bat too (laite.) Strike one! On the next (plae,) I cracked the ball hard. I didn't (wate) to see where the ball landed. I ran to first base. I was (saif!)

came	late	wait
take	play	safe

53

Answer Key

Spelling Words

cry	cry
pine	pine
light	light
nice	nice
why	why
find	find
right	right
spy	spy
spider	spider
night	night

54

Words in Context
Write the missing spelling words.

| Challenge |
| Circle the other words in the story with the /ī/ sound. |

Lost in the Woods

Once, a princess was lost in the woods at _____**night**_____.

It was so dark that she could not see any _____**light**_____. The

princess shook with (fright.) She went to (hide) under a

_____**pine**_____ tree and began to _____**cry**_____.

Suddenly, she heard a (tiny) voice.

"_____**Why**_____ are you (crying)?" asked the voice.

"Who's there?" (cried) the princess. "Are you

(trying) to _____**spy**_____ on me?"

"No, I am just a (shy) _____**spider**_____ who

lives in a web in the woods," said the voice. "(I) can

help you _____**find**_____ your way home."

The spider dropped down _____**right**_____

in front of the princess. She looked at it for a minute. "That is very

_____**nice**_____ of you," she (finally) said. " I don't know why so

many people are afraid of (spiders.)

55

Fun with Words
Write the spelling word that fits part of each rhyme.

1. The little rabbit might
   go for a hop at _____**night**_____.

2. That book was so _____**nice**_____
   that I read it twice!

3. I think you will _____**find**_____
   that it's great to be kind.

4. It is very bright
   when we turn on the _____**light**_____.

Words Across the Curriculum
Say each math word. Then, write each word.

1. line _____**line**_____   3. minus _____**minus**_____
2. wide _____**wide**_____   4. pint _____**pint**_____

Write the missing math words.

1. Nine _____**minus**_____ five equals four.
2. One _____**pint**_____ is half a quart.
3. A straight _____**line**_____ connects two points.
4. You can measure how _____**wide**_____ a box is.

56

Words in Writing
Write a fairy tale. Use at least three
words from the box.

| cry | light | why | right | spider | line | minus |
| pine | nice | find | spy | night | wide | pint |

Answers will vary.

Dictionary Practice
Circle the word in each set that comes first in ABC order. Then, write it
on the line.

1. why   (went)   wolf   _____**went**_____
2. cry   cup   (clip)   _____**clip**_____
3. not   (new)   nice   _____**new**_____
4. spy   stop   (soft)   _____**soft**_____

57

Answer Key

Say each word. Listen for the long **o** sound. Write the word.

Spelling Tip	The long **o** sound can be spelled **oa**, **o-consonant-e**, and **ow**. The sign for the long **o** sound is /ō/.

Spelling Words

own	own
coat	coat
woke	woke
flow	flow
toad	toad
row	row
those	those
road	road
slow	slow
float	float

58

Write the missing spelling words.

Challenge
Circle the other words in the story with the /ō/ sound.

On the River

Aunt (Rose) has her ___own___ cabin. Just down the ___road___ from her cabin is a river. Aunt (Rose) takes me out on the river in her boat. Sometimes, we use paddles to ___row___ the (boat.) When we want to ___slow___ down, we just let the (boat) ___float___ and watch the river ___flow___. Once, I saw a brown ___toad___ sleeping near the river. A flock of (crows) landed nearby and ___woke___ up the (toad.) (I hoped) ___those___ (crows) would leave it (alone.) The (toad) hopped away and hid under a (stone.)

Word Building
Some words sound the same but have different spellings and meanings. Write each word from the box next to the word that sounds the same.

hey	sale	rode	rose

1. road ___rode___   3. sail ___sale___
2. rows ___rose___   4. hay ___hey___

59

Fun with Words
Write the spelling words that complete the rhymes.

1. You can ___row___ a boat,
   or just let it ___float___.
2. Did you see the toad by the side of the ___road___?
3. You can stop and go and move fast or ___slow___.
4. When you are alone, you're on your ___own___.
5. The water will ___flow___ and make the plants grow.

Words Across the Curriculum
Say each science word. Then, write each word.

1. grow ___grow___   3. rose ___rose___
2. soap ___soap___   4. goat ___goat___

Write each science word next to its definition.

1. a flower with thorns on its stem ___rose___
2. to get bigger and older ___grow___
3. a farm animal that eats grass ___goat___
4. a bar that makes suds for washing ___soap___

60

Words in Writing
Write a paragraph about a person you like to visit. Use at least three of the words from the box.

own	woke	toad	those	slow	grow	rose
coat	flow	row	road	float	soap	goat

Answers will vary.

Misspelled Words
Circle the word in each set that is spelled correctly. Then, write it on the line.

1. flote   flowt   (float)   ___float___
2. owne   (own)   oan   ___own___
3. (toad)   tode   towd   ___toad___
4. floe   (flow)   flowe   ___flow___
5. (row)   rowe   roe   ___row___
6. sloe   slowe   (slow)   ___slow___

61

Answer Key

Say each word. Listen for the /ü/ sound. Write the word.

Spelling Tip	The /ü/ sound can be spelled **oo** and **u-consonant-e**.

Spelling Words

too	too
rude	rude
room	room
zoo	zoo
glue	glue
soon	soon
cool	cool
moon	moon
food	food
pool	pool

62

Words in Context
Write the missing spelling words.

Challenge
Circle the other words in the description with the /ü/ sound.

Otters

I like to see otters at the ____zoo____. They splash and fool around in their ____pool____, even when it's ____cool____ outside. They zoom down their slide, too. Sometimes, the otters are ____rude____ to each other. One otter sometimes steals a small piece of ____food____ from another otter. Then, it runs into a ____room____ in their shelter and hides. The otters play until the ____moon____ comes out at night. I hope to visit them ____soon____.

Word Building
sun + shine = sunshine

A compound word is made of two smaller words. Write the spelling word that goes with each word. Then, write the compound word.

1. bed + ____room____ = ____bedroom____
2. ____zoo____ + keeper = ____zookeeper____
3. ____moon____ + light = ____moonlight____

63

Fun with Words
Subtract and add letters to make spelling words.

1. coop – p + l = ____cool____
2. fool – l + d = ____food____
3. rule – l + d = ____rude____
4. noon – n + s = ____soon____
5. gloom – oom + ue = ____glue____
6. loom – l + r = ____room____
7. moo – m + z = ____zoo____
8. spool – s = ____pool____

Words Across the Curriculum
Say each art word. Then, write each word.

1. tune ____tune____
2. tube ____tube____

Write the missing art words.

3. Paint can come in a jar or a ____tube____.
4. The band played a happy ____tune____.

64

Words in Writing
Write a list of rules for school, home, or another place. Use at least three words from the box.

too	room	glue	cool	food	tune
rude	zoo	soon	moon	pool	tube

Answers will vary.

Misspelled Words
Read the student's list of rules. Circle the five misspelled words. Then, write the words correctly.

1. Do not run near the poole. ____pool____
2. Keep all fude away from the water. ____food____
3. Get out of the water as sune as the lifeguards blow their whistles. ____soon____
4. Don't be rood to the lifeguards. ____rude____
5. Keep the dressing rome clean. ____room____

65

Page 66

Say each word. Listen for the long **e** sound. Write the word.

Spelling Tip	The long **e** sound can be spelled **e**, **ee** and **ea**. The sign for the long **e** sound is /ē/.

Spelling Words

eat	eat
meet	meet
team	team
keep	keep
each	each
leave	leave
read	read
teeth	teeth
sleep	sleep
clean	clean

66

Page 67

Words in Context
Write the missing spelling words.

Challenge
Circle the other words in the description with the /ē/ sound.

Saturdays

Saturday is a busy day for me. After I brush my _____ **teeth** _____ and _____ **eat** _____ breakfast, I have to _____ **clean** _____ my room. I have to _____ **keep** _____ working until it's time for lunch. After lunch, I _____ **leave** _____ my house to go to my soccer game. I _____ **meet** _____ the players on my soccer _____ **team** _____ at the field. _____ **Each** _____ one of us has to run at least three laps before our game. After we play our game, I usually go to a movie. Before I go to _____ **sleep** _____, I _____ **read** _____ a book and have a cup of hot tea.

Word Building
Add the **-ing** ending to make new words.

1. eat **ing**
2. read **ing**
3. meet **ing**
4. keep **ing**
5. clean **ing**
6. sleep **ing**

67

Page 68

Fun with Words
Write the spelling word that fits each sentence and rhymes with each underlined word.

1. We <u>need</u> to _____ **read** _____ a book each week.
2. This group of players <u>seem</u> to be a <u>dream</u> _____ **team** _____.
3. I counted <u>sheep</u> to help me _____ **sleep** _____.
4. I sat on my <u>seat</u> to _____ **eat** _____ my <u>meat</u>.
5. I can <u>reach</u> _____ **each** _____ <u>peach</u> on the tree.
6. Do you <u>greet</u> everyone you _____ **meet** _____?

Words Across the Curriculum
Say each math word. Then, each word.

1. week _____ **week** _____
2. meter _____ **meter** _____
3. equal _____ **equal** _____
4. even _____ **even** _____

Write the missing math words.

1. Three plus three is _____ **equal** _____ to six.
2. A _____ **meter** _____ is a metric unit of length.
3. Two, four, and six are _____ **even** _____ numbers.
4. There are seven days in one _____ **week** _____.

68

Page 69

Words in Writing
Make a list of things that you do on weekends. Use at least three words from the box.

eat	team	each	read	sleep	week	equal
meet	keep	leave	teeth	clean	meter	even

_____

_____

_____

Answers will vary.

Misspelled Words
Read the student's list of things to do. Circle the seven misspelled words. Then, write the words correctly.

1. Brush my teath. — **teeth**
2. Cleen my room, and put eech toy away. — **clean** / **each**
3. Practice soccer with the players on my teem. — **team**
4. Reed a book. — **Read**
5. Meete my sister for lunch. — **Meet**
6. I will eet a snack with my tea. — **eat**

69

Answer Key

Answer Key

Fun with Words

Write the spelling words that complete the comparisons.

1. **Dig** is to **shovel** as **sweep** is to _____broom_____ .

2. **Dark** is to **night** as _____bright_____ is to **light**.

3. **Crayon** is to **color** as _____brush_____ is to **paint**.

4. **Top** is to **bottom** as _____front_____ is to **back**.

5. **Open** is to **close** as _____free_____ is to **trap**.

6. **Snake** is to **slither** as _____frog_____ is to **hop**.

Words Across the Curriculum

Say each science word. Then, write each word.

1. frost _____frost_____   3. fruit _____fruit_____

2. brick _____brick_____   4. breeze _____breeze_____

Write each science word next to the pair of words it belongs with.

1. stone, wood, _____brick_____

2. apple, orange, _____fruit_____

3. snow, ice, _____frost_____

4. wind, air, _____breeze_____

74

Words in Writing

Write a paragraph that tells about an animal. Use at least three of the words from the box.

free	from	break	broom	front	frost	fruit
bright	brush	frog	fresh	bread	brick	breeze

Answers will vary.

Misspelled Words

Read the student's description of an animal. Circle the four misspelled words. Then, write the words correctly.

    I found a (frogg) at the pond. I named him Freddie. Freddie's skin is (brite) green. He has brown spots on the (frunt) of his legs. I decided not to take Freddie from the pond. Freddie needs to be free. He likes to sit by the pond and feel the (breze) on his skin.

_____frog_____   _____front_____

_____bright_____   _____breeze_____

75

Say each word. Listen to the beginning sound. Write the word.

Spelling Tip	The /sl/ and /sp/ sounds are spelled **sl** and **sp**.

Spelling Words

spin	_____spin_____
slip	_____slip_____
slam	_____slam_____
sled	_____sled_____
speak	_____speak_____
slide	_____slide_____
sport	_____sport_____
spill	_____spill_____
spoon	_____spoon_____
slice	_____slice_____

76

Words in Context

Write the missing spelling words.

Challenge
Circle the other words in the description with **sl** and **sp**.

Winter Fun

    In winter, I like to (speed) down a snowy hill on my _____sled_____ . I go so fast I can't stop to _____speak_____ to my friends who are on the (slope.) Ice-skating is another fun winter _____sport_____ . Sometimes, I _____spin_____ in a circle on the ice. Then, I _____slide_____ on the ice as fast as I can. I try not to _____slam_____ into other skaters. When I go over a (slick) (spot) on the ice, sometimes I _____slip_____ and fall. When I get too cold, I go inside. I have a _____slice_____ of pizza and a bowl of hot soup. My hands are so cold I have to grip my _____spoon_____ so I don't _____spill_____ my soup.

Word Building

Write the word from the box that tells about the past.

1. Today, I **spin**. Yesterday, I _____spun_____ .

2. Today, I **speak**. Yesterday, I _____spoke_____ .

spoke
spun

77

Answer Key

Page 78

Fun with Words

Fill in the missing vowels to make the spelling words.

1. sp__o__ __o__ n
2. sl__e__ d
3. sl__i__ d __e__
4. sp__i__ ll
5. sl__a__ m
6. sl__i__ c __e__
7. sl__i__ p
8. sp__o__ rt
9. sp__e__ __a__ k
10. sp__i__ n

Words Across the Curriculum

Say each art word. Then, write each word.

1. slant ___slant___
2. slit ___slit___
3. space ___space___
4. spray ___spray___

Write the missing art words.

1. You can brush or ___spray___ paint on a work of art.
2. Zigzag lines ___slant___ from one side to another.
3. To make a mask, cut one ___slit___ for each eye.
4. It's good to leave some empty ___space___ in a painting.

78

Page 79

Words in Writing

Write about what you like to do outside in winter. Use at least three of the words from the box.

| spin | slam | speak | sport | spoon | slant | space |
| slip | sled | slide | spill | slice | slit | spray |

Answers will vary.

Dictionary Practice

To find a word in a dictionary, you sometimes have to look at the second letter of the words on a page. Circle the second letter in each word. Then, write the words in ABC order.

1. (s)l(i)de
2. st(i)ck
3. s(h)ow
4. s(m)all
5. s(w)eep
6. s(k)ip
7. s(p)in
8. s(n)ake

1. ___show___
2. ___skip___
3. ___slide___
4. ___small___
5. ___snake___
6. ___spin___
7. ___stick___
8. ___sweep___

79

Page 80

Say each word. Listen to the beginning sound. Write the word.

| Spelling Tip | The /sh/ and /wh/ sounds are often spelled **sh** and **wh**. |

Spelling Words

whip	___whip___
shoe	___shoe___
shall	___shall___
wheel	___wheel___
share	___share___
shine	___shine___
while	___while___
shake	___shake___
where	___where___
which	___which___

80

Page 81

Words in Context

Write the missing spelling words.

Challenge

Circle the other words in the story with **sh** and **wh**.

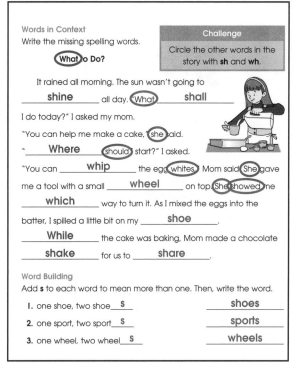

(What) to Do?

It rained all morning. The sun wasn't going to ___shine___ all day. (What) ___shall___ I do today?" I asked my mom.

"You can help me make a cake," (she) said.

"___Where___ (should) I start?" I asked.

"You can ___whip___ the egg (whites). Mom said (She) gave me a tool with a small ___wheel___ on top. (She) (showed) me ___which___ way to turn it. As I mixed the eggs into the batter, I spilled a little bit on my ___shoe___.

___While___ the cake was baking, Mom made a chocolate ___shake___ for us to ___share___.

Word Building

Add **s** to each word to mean more than one. Then, write the word.

1. one shoe, two shoe__s__   ___shoes___
2. one sport, two sport__s__   ___sports___
3. one wheel, two wheel__s__   ___wheels___

81

Answer Key

Page 82

Fun with Words

Unscramble the letters to make the spelling words.

1. lashl   shall   6. phiw   whip
2. sneih   shine   7. rheas   share
3. ekahs   shake   8. lhewi   while
4. ehwer   where   9. elweh   wheel
5. oesh   shoe   10. ciwhh   which

Words Across the Curriculum

Say each science word. Then, write each word.

1. shore   shore   3. shadow   shadow
2. wheat   wheat   4. shade   shade

Write the science word next to the place in which you can find it.

1. in a field   wheat
2. under a tree   shade
3. behind you   shadow
4. next to a lake   shore

82

Page 83

Words in Writing

What kind of party would you like to have? Write an invitation to a party. Use at least three of the words from the box.

| whip | shall | share | while | where | shore | shadow |
| shoe | wheel | shine | shade | which | wheat | shade |

Answers will vary.

Misspelled Words

Read the invitation. Circle the five misspelled words. Then, write the words correctly on the lines below.

When: 2:00 on Saturday, May 3, rain or (shene)
(Wheer)   At the park near the (shoar) of the lake
Given by: Mia

P.S. Please bring a snack to (sheare). (I shal) bring everything else.

shine   shore   shall
Where   share

83

Page 84

Say each word. Listen for the **ch** and **th** sounds. Write the word.

| Spelling Tip | The /ch/ and /th/ sounds are often spelled **ch** and **th**. |

Spelling Words

with   with
such   such
think   think
both   both
chase   chase
reach   reach
thing   thing
teach   teach
catch   catch
child   child

84

Page 85

Words in Context

Write the missing spelling words.

Challenge

Circle the other words in the story with **ch** and **th**.

Soccer Is Fun!

Do you like to play soccer? It's _____ such _____ a fun sport! I _____ think _____ (that) every _____ child _____ should learn how to play. Most (coaches) _____ teach _____ (their) players to kick and trap (the) ball with _____ both _____ feet (They) also tell (the) players to stay in (their) positions and not _____ chase _____ (the) ball all over (the field (Another) _____ thing _____ players have to remember is not to _____ reach _____ for (the) ball _____ with _____ (their) hands. Only (the) goalkeeper can use his hands to _____ catch _____ (the) ball.

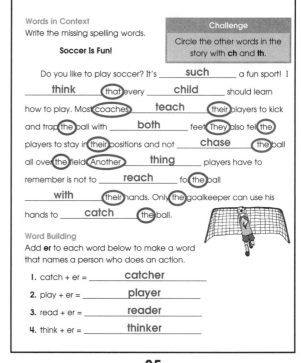

Word Building

Add **er** to each word below to make a word that names a person who does an action.

1. catch + er =   catcher
2. play + er =   player
3. read + er =   reader
4. think + er =   thinker

85

Answer Key

Fun with Words

Add **ch** or **th** to make the spelling words that rhyme.

1. match, cat__ch__   5. wild, __ch__ild
2. base, __ch__ase   6. much, su__ch__
3. ring, __th__ing   7. pink, __th__ink
4. peach, rea__ch__   8. beach, tea__ch__

Words Across the Curriculum

Say each math word. Then, write each word.

1. inch __inch__   3. change __change__
2. month __month__   4. width __width__

Write each math word next to the word it is like.

1. money __change__
2. distance across __width__
3. length __inch__
4. week __month__

86

Words in Writing

What is your favorite sport? Write a paragraph that tells how to play the sport. Use at least three of the words from the box.

_____

_____

Answers will vary.

| with | think | chase | thing | catch | inch | change |
| such | both | reach | teach | child | month | width |

Dictionary Practice

A dictionary has guide words at the top of the page. All the words on the page come between the guide words in ABC order. Write the word from the box that comes between each pair of guide words.

1. wash __width__ wise
2. take __teach__ thing
3. bath __both__ bring
4. ship __such__ swim
5. race __reach__ rich

87

Write the spelling word that has the same meaning.

1. turn __spin__
2. shiver __shake__
3. grab __catch__
4. glow __shine__
5. cut __slice__
6. will __shall__
7. game __sport__
8. beat __whip__

Write the spelling word that rhymes with each pair of words.

1. log, fog, __frog__
2. jam, dam, __slam__
3. make, rake, __shake__
4. moon, noon, __spoon__
5. meal, peel, __wheel__
6. light, night, __bright__
7. ride, hide, __slide__
8. beak, week, __speak__

88

Write the spelling word that means the opposite.

1. dull __bright__
2. throw __catch__
3. back __front__
4. fix __break__
5. to __from__
6. capture __free__

Write the spelling words that fit the questions.

1. __Where__ are you going?
2. Did you sweep the floor with the __broom__ ?
3. Did you hear the door __slam__ ?
4. Can I __brush__ your hair for you?
5. __Which__ book should we read?
6. Would you like to __share__ my lunch with me?
7. May I have some jam on my __bread__ ?
8. Can I ride your __sled__ down the hill?

89

Answer Key

Say each word. Listen for the /är/ sound. Write the word.

Spelling Tip	The /är/ sound is often spelled **ar**.

Spelling Words

far	far
farm	farm
yard	yard
cart	cart
hard	hard
park	park
start	start
part	part
sharp	sharp
garden	garden

90

Words in Context
Write the missing spelling words.

Farm Work

Challenge
Circle the other words in the story with the /är/ sound.

There is a lot of ____ hard ____ work to do on a ____ farm ____. You have to set you(alarm)early and then ____ start ____ working. First, you feed the animals. Then, you let them out of the(barn)You have to make sure they don't go ____ far ____ from the ____ yard ____. This is only ____ part ____ of the day's work. There(are)more chores outside in the ____ garden ____. You have to dig up weeds with a ____ sharp ____ tool. Then, you wheel them away in a ____ cart ____. It's much(harder)to work on a(farm)than in a ____ park ____!

Word Building
The ending **-er** can compare two things. Add **er** to make a new word that compares. Then, write the new word.

1. This tack is **sharp**. That tack is **sharp**__er__.   sharper
2. This job is **hard**. That job is **hard**__er__.   harder
3. This dog is **smart**. That dog is **smart**__er__.   smarter

91

Fun with Words
Write the spelling word that completes each rhyme.

1. Don't let the dog bark when he runs in the ____ park ____.
2. It's not very hard to work in the ____ yard ____.
3. It's time to ____ start ____ on a work of art.
4. An actor who's smart will play a good ____ part ____.
5. You can go very ____ far ____ when you drive in a car.
6. You must have a strong arm to work on a ____ farm ____.

Words Across the Curriculum
Say each art word. Then, write each word.

1. art   art   3. carve   carve
2. dark   dark   4. mark   mark

Write the art words to complete the directions.

Here's how to make a jack'o'lantern from a pumpkin. First, use a ____ dark ____ pen to ____ mark ____ the parts of the face. Then, have an adult use a knife to ____ carve ____ them out. If you do a good job, you will have a work of ____ art ____!

92

Words in Writing
Have you ever had a dog for a pet? Write a list of things to do to take care of a dog. Use at least three of the words from the box.

| far | yard | hard | start | sharp | art | carve |
| farm | cart | park | part | garden | dart | mark |

Answers will vary.

Misspelled Words
Read the list of things to do to take care of a dog. Circle the five misspelled words. Then, write the words correctly.

1. Let the dog play in the(yerd).   yard
2. Don't let her dig in the(gerden).   garden
3. Cut her nails when they start to get too(sharpe) sharp
4. Take her for walks in the(parck).   park
5. Don't let her get too(fare)away.   far

93

Answer Key

Say each word. Listen for the /ôr/ and /ûr/ sounds. Write the word.

Spelling Tip	The /ôr/ sound can be spelled **ir** or **ur**. The /ûr/ sound can be spelled **or**.

Spelling Words

girl	girl
fort	fort
turn	turn
first	first
more	more
hurt	hurt
dirt	dirt
store	store
short	short
burn	burn

94

Words in Context
Write the missing spelling words.

Challenge
Circle the other words in the letter with the /ôr/ and /ûr/ sounds.

Dear (Burt),

Thank you (for) letting me stay at (your) farm last weekend. Now, it's (your) ___**turn**___ to visit me. We can shop at the new (sports) ___**store**___. It's just a ___**short**___ walk down the street. We also can play with the ___**girl**___ who lives next (door). She and I just built a ___**fort**___ in (her) yard. ___**First**___, we collected some (boards) that (her) dad didn't need. He was going to ___**burn**___ them in the fireplace. We nailed the (boards) together to make the (fort). I ___**hurt**___ my finger with the hammer, but it's not too (sore). We packed the ___**dirt**___ down hard to make a (floor). I'll tell you ___**more**___ about the (fort) the next time I write.

Your friend,
Mario

95

Fun with Words
Write the spelling word that completes each tongue-twister.

1. Steve's ___**store**___ still sells stickers.
2. Dad doesn't dig ___**dirt**___ during the day.
3. Tim took a ___**turn**___ telling a tall tale.
4. Mary must make ___**more**___ money.
5. Greta is a ___**girl**___ who gets good grades.
6. Sue shall show Shellie the six ___**short**___ sheep.

Words Across the Curriculum
Say each science word. Then, write each word.

1. bird ___**bird**___   3. north ___**north**___
2. horse ___**horse**___   4. turtle ___**turtle**___

Write each science word next to the group of words it belongs with.

1. south, east, west, ___**north**___
2. lizard, snake, alligator, ___**turtle**___
3. zebra, mule, pony, ___**horse**___
4. robin, eagle, owl, ___**bird**___

96

Words in Writing
Write the directions to a place near your home. Use at least three words from the box.

girl	turn	more	dirt	short	bird	north
fort	first	hurt	store	burn	horse	turtle

Answers will vary.

Misspelled Words
Circle the correct spelling for each word.

1. furst   forst   (first)   ___**first**___
2. (hurt)   hirt   hort   ___**hurt**___
3. (store)   stor   sture   ___**store**___
4. tirn   (turn)   turne   ___**turn**___
5. shurt   (short)   shirte   ___**short**___
6. (burn)   birn   burne   ___**burn**___

97

Answer Key

Say each word. Listen for the /s/ and /z/sounds. Write the word.

Spelling Tip	The /s/ sound can be spelled **s** or **ce**. The /z/ sound can be spelled **se**.

Spelling Words

once	once
use	use
race	race
nose	nose
nice	nice
please	please
mouse	mouse
place	place
house	house
because	because

98

Words in Context
Write the missing spelling words.

Challenge
Circle the other words in the story with **ce** and **se**.

My Pet Mike

I have a pet ___mouse___ named Mike. He has a gray body with white spots on his (race). He also has a long, pointed ___nose___. At first, my mom didn't want him in the ___house___. I had to beg her to ___please___ let me keep Mike. When she saw how ___nice___ he is, my mom said yes. ___Once___, Mike got (loose) ___because___ I forgot to (close) his cage door. I had to ___race___ after him. He ran all over the ___place___. I finally (chased) him into a corner. Then, I had to ___use___ a net to catch him. It's a good thing my mom wasn't home!

99

Fun with Words
Add **se** or **ce** to make the spelling words.

1. hou **se**
2. becau **se**
3. no **se**
4. ra **ce**
5. u **se**
6. ni **ce**
7. mou **se**
8. on **ce**
9. pla **ce**
10. plea **se**

Words Across the Curriculum
Say each art word. Then, write each word.

1. dance ___dance___
2. pose ___pose___
3. pencil ___pencil___
4. paste ___paste___

Write the art word that completes each sentence.

1. Will you ___pose___ for me so I can paint a picture of you?
2. I used a ___pencil___ to sketch the house.
3. It's fun to sing and ___dance___.
4. You can ___paste___ cutout shapes on a sheet of paper.

100

Words in Writing
Write a description of a piece of art you made. Use at least three of the words from the box.

once	race	nice	mouse	house	dance	pencil
use	nose	please	place	because	pose	paste

Answers will vary.

Dictionary Practice
A dictionary has a beginning, middle, and end. Write ten spelling words where you would find them in the dictionary.

ABCDEFGH	IJKLMNOPQ	RSTUVWXYZ
because	mouse	race
house	nice	use
	nose	
	once	
	place	
	please	

101

Spectrum Spelling
Grade 2
184

Answer Key

Answer Key

Page 102

Write the spelling word that means the opposite.

1. easy   **hard**
2. last   **first**
3. tall   **short**
4. boy   **girl**
5. stop   **start**
6. dull   **sharp**
7. less   **more**
8. mean   **nice**
9. near   **far**
10. whole   **part**

Write the spelling word that names a place where you would find each thing.

1. flowers   **garden**
2. bedroom   **house**
3. soldiers   **fort**
4. crops   **farm**

102

Page 103

Write the spelling word that tells about each action.

1. You can **park** a car in a lot.
2. You can **use** a pencil to draw a picture.
3. You can **race** with other runners.
4. You can **burn** your finger on a hot stove.

Write the spelling word that completes each sentence.

1. I stayed in bed today **because** I was sick.
2. Go down the hall and **turn** left at the second door.
3. May I **please** see your new book?
4. I like to play with my friends at the **park**.
5. My mom pushed the shopping **cart** through the store.
6. Did you **hurt** your foot when you stepped on the tack?
7. My cat chased a **mouse** in the yard.
8. **Once**, I saw a shooting star in the sky.

103

Page 104

Say each word. Look at the two letters before the **-s** or **-es** ending. Write the word.

Spelling Tip	Add **s** or **es** to most nouns to mean more than one. When a word ends with **s, ss, ch, sh** or **x**, add **-es**.

Spelling Words

students	**students**
foxes	**foxes**
bushes	**bushes**
watches	**watches**
beaches	**beaches**
branches	**branches**
classes	**classes**
books	**books**
flashes	**flashes**
animals	**animals**

104

Page 105

Words in Context
Write the missing spelling words.

A Fun Day

Challenge
Circle the other words in the story that mean more than one.

Yesterday, the **students** at our school had a fun day. We didn't stay in our (rooms) and we didn't read any **books**. We didn't have any **classes** at all. Instead, we rode in (buses) to the lake. We rode past a few **beaches** before we stopped to go swimming. We changed our (clothes) and took off our **watches**. We left them under some **bushes** and went swimming. After a few (hours) it started to rain. We saw some **flashes** of lightning behind some tree **branches**. Soon, the rain stopped. We hiked through the forest by the lake to look for **animals**. We saw a lot of (birds) and (squirrels) We even saw two red **foxes**.

105

Spectrum Spelling
Grade 2

Answer Key

Fun with Words
Circle the hidden spelling words.

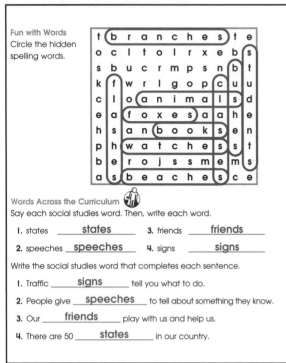

Words Across the Curriculum
Say each social studies word. Then, write each word.

1. states _____states_____   3. friends _____friends_____

2. speeches _____speeches_____   4. signs _____signs_____

Write the social studies word that completes each sentence.

1. Traffic _____signs_____ tell you what to do.

2. People give _____speeches_____ to tell about something they know.

3. Our _____friends_____ play with us and help us.

4. There are 50 _____states_____ in our country.

106

Words in Writing
Write a paragraph that tells what you do on the weekends. Use at least three words from the box.

| students | bushes | beaches | classes | flashes | states | friends |
| foxes | watches | branches | books | animals | speeches | signs |

Answers will vary.

Misspelled Words
Read the paragraph. Circle the four misspelled words. Then, write the words correctly on the lines below.

On the weekends, there are no school clases. I help my dad clean our house. I also help him cut the grass and trim the buches in the yard. We leave some food out for the wild animals. Then, I play outside with my friendes. When we get tired, we go inside and read bookes.

_____classes_____   _____friends_____

_____bushes_____   _____books_____

107

Say each word. Listen to the ending sound. Write the word.

| Spelling Tip | For some words with only one vowel, double the last consonant before adding **ed** or **ing**. |

Spelling Words

winning _____winning_____

tapped _____tapped_____

clapping _____clapping_____

digging _____digging_____

slipped _____slipped_____

stepped _____stepped_____

running _____running_____

dropped _____dropped_____

skipped _____skipped_____

hugged _____hugged_____

108

Words in Context
Write the missing spelling words.

The Last Inning

Challenge
Circle the other words in the story that have double consonants before **ed** or **ing**.

The baseball game was in the last inning. The Tigers' best batter was next. He _____stepped_____ up to the plate. He looked down and started _____digging_____ the toe of his shoe into the dirt. Then he looked up at the pitcher and gripped his bat with both hands. He gently _____tapped_____ the first pitch with his bat and started _____running_____ to first base. The ball popped out to left field. The outfielder held out his mitt, but then his feet _____slipped_____ on the wet grass. He _____dropped_____ the ball! The runner on third base _____skipped_____ to home plate. The other players on his team ran out and _____hugged_____ him. The fans started _____clapping_____ and hopping up and down. The Tigers still had their _____winning_____ streak.

109

Answer Key

Fun with Words

Write the spelling word that rhymes with the underlined word and fits in each sentence.

1. I ___dropped___ the chips that I had <u>chopped</u>.

2. The ___winning___ players were all <u>grinning</u>.

3. I <u>tripped</u> and fell as I ___slipped___ down the road.

4. The fans were ___clapping___ and <u>tapping</u> their feet.

5. The baby's mom ___hugged___ him when he <u>tugged</u> on her dress.

6. The stick <u>snapped</u> in two when I ___tapped___ it on the floor.

Words Across the Curriculum

Say each art word. Then, write each word.

1. cutting ___cutting___ 3. dipped ___dipped___

2. hummed ___hummed___ 4. dripping ___dripping___

Write the missing art words.

1. Some people make artwork by ___dripping___ paint onto paper.

2. Be careful when you're ___cutting___ paper with scissors.

3. I ___dipped___ my brush into the blue paint.

4. The boy ___hummed___ a tune to himself.

110

Words in Writing

What sport do you like to watch? Write a description of a sports game you watched. Use at least three words from the box.

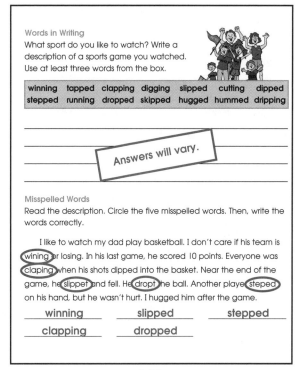

| winning | tapped | clapping | digging | slipped | cutting | dipped |
| stepped | running | dropped | skipped | hugged | hummed | dripping |

_____

Answers will vary.

Misspelled Words

Read the description. Circle the five misspelled words. Then, write the words correctly.

I like to watch my dad play basketball. I don't care if his team is (wining) or losing. In his last game, he scored 10 points. Everyone was (claping) when his shots dipped into the basket. Near the end of the game, he (slippet) and fell. He (dropt) the ball. Another player (steped) on his hand, but he wasn't hurt. I hugged him after the game.

___winning___ ___slipped___ ___stepped___

___clapping___ ___dropped___

111

Say each word. Look at the spelling. Write the word.

| **Spelling Tip** | Some words aren't spelled the way they sound. You have to remember how to spell them. |

Spelling Words

our	___our___
give	___give___
very	___very___
new	___new___
were	___were___
goes	___goes___
many	___many___
next	___next___
why	___why___
every	___every___

112

Words in Context

Write the missing spelling words.

Yard Sale

> **Challenge**
> Circle the three words in the ad that have a **vowel-consonant-e** pattern but a short vowel sound.

Our class is having a yard sale ___next___ week. We will (have) ___many___ toys and clothes that ___were___ used only once or twice. We'll also (have) (some) ___new___ ones. ___Every___ item will (have) a ___very___ low price. We'll ___give___ you free cookies and juice just for coming to ___our___ sale. The sale ___goes___ on all day. ___Why___ don't you plan to (come?)

Word Building

Add **s** to each pronoun to show that something belongs to a person or animal. Then, write the word.

1. This is our house. This house is our_**s**_. ___ours___

2. The dog is happy. It is wagging it_**s**_ tail. ___its___

3. Rosa found her coat. That coat is her_**s**_. ___hers___

4. Is this your pencil? I think it is your_**s**_. ___yours___

113

Answer Key

Fun with Words

Write the spelling word that fits in each pattern.

1. go, __goes__, going
2. one, few, __many__, most
3. each, all, __every__
4. first, __next__, last
5. is, are, __were__
6. my, your, __our__
7. __new__, used, old
8. who, what, __why__

Words Across the Curriculum

Say each math word. Then, write each word.

1. cube __cube__
2. money __money__
3. length __length__
4. circle __circle__

Write the math word that completes each sentence.

1. Inches and meters measure __length__.
2. A __circle__ is a closed, curved line.
3. __Money__ is used to buy things.
4. Most blocks have the shape of a __cube__.

114

Words in Writing

Write the words for a poster that tell about a yard sale. Use at least three words from the box.

| our | very | were | many | why | cube | length |
| give | new | goes | next | every | money | circle |

Answers will vary.

Dictionary Practice

Circle the word that comes between each pair of guide words in ABC order.

1. orange—our   oven   open   (otter)
2. were—who   why   (when)   woke
3. under—wait   stop   way   (very)
4. many—most   (milk)   must   my
5. next—now   napkin   (night)   nest
6. circle—cry   cube   (come)   cuddle

115

Write the spelling word that rhymes with each word.

1. stopped __dropped__
2. boxes __foxes__
3. live __give__
4. try __why__
5. looks __books__
6. tugged __hugged__
7. rapped __tapped__
8. dashes __flashes__
9. berry __very__
10. glasses __classes__

Write the spelling word that means the opposite.

1. losing __winning__
2. none __every__
3. old __new__
4. few __many__

116

Write the spelling word that means the same or almost the same.

1. shores __beaches__
2. walked __stepped__
3. slid __slipped__
4. clocks __watches__
5. each __every__
6. shrubs __bushes__

Write the spelling word that completes each sentence.

1. You can see __animals__ at the zoo.
2. The girls __were__ there when I got home.
3. The birds are sitting on the __branches__ of the tree.
4. The fans are __clapping__ for their team.
5. I am the __next__ person in line.
6. My dog is __digging__ a hole in the yard.

117

Answer Key

Page 118

Say each word. Notice the different spellings of the words that sound the same. Write each word.

Spelling Tip — Some words sound the same but have different spellings and meanings.

Spelling Words

meat	meat
deer	deer
hole	hole
road	road
dear	dear
there	there
whole	whole
meet	meet
rode	rode
their	their

118

Page 119

Words in Context
Write the missing spelling words.

_____Dear_____ Mom,

I'm having a (great) time at Uncle Pete's ranch. Yesterday, we _____rode_____ horses along a dirt _____road_____. We were on (our) way (to) _____meet_____ (some) friends of Uncle (Pete). _____Their_____ ranch is only a few miles away. On the way _____there_____ (I) saw a _____deer_____ hiding in the trees. It tripped over a _____hole_____ in the ground as it ran away. When we got (to) the ranch, Uncle (Pete) and (I) had lunch. (I) ate a _____whole_____ plate of _____meat_____ and vegetables. I'll (write) again soon.

Love,
Irene

Challenge
Circle the words in the letter that sound the same as the words **eye, sum, too, right, hour, peat,** and **grate.**

Word Building
Add **er** and **est** to make new words that compare.

1. dear, dear__er__, dear__est__
2. long, long__er__, long__est__

119

Page 120

Fun with Words
Write the spelling word that rhymes and has the same spelling pattern.

1. code _____rode_____   4. near _____dear_____
2. seat _____meat_____   5. load _____road_____
3. where _____there_____   6. mole _____hole_____

Words Across the Curriculum
Say each science word. Then, write each word.

1. sea _____sea_____   3. eye _____eye_____
2. hear _____hear_____   4. hour _____hour_____

Write the science word next to its definition. Then, write a word that sounds the same but has a different spelling and meaning. Use the dictionary in the back if you need help.

1. listen _____hear_____ _____here_____
2. 60 minutes _____hour_____ _____our_____
3. ocean _____sea_____ _____see_____
4. body part that lets you see _____eye_____ _____I_____

120

Page 121

Words in Writing
Write an ad for a restaurant where you like to eat. Use at least three words from the box.

meat	hole	dear	whole	rode	sea	eye
deer	road	there	meet	their	hear	hour

Answers will vary.

Incorrect Words
Read the ad. Circle the six words that are used incorrectly for their meaning. Then, write the correct words.

Did you (here) about Mia's Place yet? You can get great food (their). You can get a (hole) pizza for just five dollars. You can get (meet) or vegetable toppings for free. It's a fun place to (meat) your friends. It's right on the beach, next to the (see.)

hear	whole	meet
there	meat	sea

121

Answer Key

Answer Key

Say each word. Look at the spelling of each word. Write each word.

Spelling Tip	Many family words don't fit a spelling pattern. You have to remember how to spell them.

Spelling Words

family	family
mother	mother
father	father
sister	sister
brother	brother
baby	baby
aunt	aunt
uncle	uncle
grandfather	grandfather
grandmother	grandmother

122

Words in Context
Write the missing spelling words.

Challenge
Circle the other family words in the description.

My Family

There are many people in my __family__. My __father__ is a teacher. His (parents) are my (grandparents). My __grandfather__ likes to go fishing in his boat. My __grandmother__ is a very good cook. My __mother__ is an artist. Sometimes, she paints pictures of me with my __sister__ Maria and my __brother__ Carlos. My (mother's brother) is an artist, too. He is my __uncle__. His (wife) is my __aunt__ (Uncle) Paul and (Aunt) Rita just had a __baby__. I like to hold my new (cousin).

123

Fun with Words
Write the spelling word that goes with each clue.

1. your mom — mother
2. a girl whose mom is your mom — sister
3. your dad — father
4. your dad's brother — uncle
5. your dad's sister — aunt
6. a boy whose dad is your dad — brother
7. your dad's dad — grandfather
8. your mom's mom — grandmother

Words Across the Curriculum
Say each social studies word. Then, write each word.

1. parent — parent
2. cousin — cousin
3. together — together
4. people — people

Write the social studies word or words that complete each sentence.

1. The __people__ in a family work and play __together__.
2. A __parent__ takes care of his or her children.
3. My aunt's son is my __cousin__.

124

Words in Writing
A family tree shows how the people in a family are related. Make your family tree. Use words from the box to name your family members.

_____

Answers will vary.

family	father	brother	aunt	grandfather	parent	together
mother	sister	baby	uncle	grandmother	cousin	people

Dictionary Practice
A dictionary has a beginning, middle, and end. Write the words from the box where you would find them in the dictionary.

ABCDEFGH	IJKLMNOPQ	RSTUVWXYZ
aunt	mother	sister
baby	parent	together
brother	people	uncle
cousin		
family		
father		
grandfather		
grandmother		

125

Answer Key

Say each word. Look at the spelling of each word. Write each word.

Spelling Tip	Some number words are spelled the way they sound. You have to remember how to spell others.

Spelling Words

one	one
two	two
three	three
four	four
five	five
six	six
seven	seven
eight	eight
nine	nine
ten	ten

126

Words in Context
Write the missing spelling words.

1. A person has _____five_____ fingers on one hand.
2. A person has _____ten_____ fingers altogether.
3. _____Two_____ gloves are a pair.
4. There are _____nine_____ players on a baseball team.
5. A triangle has _____three_____ sides.
6. The 50 states make _____one_____ country.
7. There are _____seven_____ days in a week.
8. A square has _____four_____ sides.
9. A cube has _____six_____ faces.
10. A spider has _____eight_____ legs.

Word Building
Some number words add **th** to make words that tell what order things are in. Add **th** to the end of each word to make a new word that tells about order. Then, write the word.

1. four___th___ _____fourth_____
2. six___th___ _____sixth_____
3. seven___th___ _____seventh_____
4. ten___th___ _____tenth_____

127

Fun with Words
Write the spelling word that rhymes with the underlined word.

1. _____Ten_____ pigs are in a <u>pen</u>.
2. _____Eight_____ geese are at the <u>gate</u>.
3. _____Six_____ sisters pick up <u>sticks</u>.
4. _____Four_____ friends are at the <u>door</u>.
5. _____Five_____ bees are in their <u>hive</u>.
6. _____Three_____ foxes are running <u>free</u>.
7. _____Two_____ circles are colored <u>blue</u>.
8. _____Nine_____ numbers are on the <u>line</u>.

Words Across the Curriculum
Say each math word. Then, write each word.

1. second _____second_____   3. fifth _____fifth_____
2. third _____third_____   4. ninth _____ninth_____

Write the math words in the correct order.

1. first, _____second_____, _____third_____, fourth
2. _____fifth_____, sixth, seventh
3. eighth, _____ninth_____, tenth

128

Words in Writing
Write a paragraph that tells about people in your family. Use at least three words from the box.

one	three	five	seven	nine	second	fifth
two	four	six	eight	ten	third	ninth

Answers will vary.

Misspelled Words
Read the paragraph. Circle the five misspelled words. Then, write the words correctly.

I am (eigth) years old. I'm in the (sicond) grade. I have one older sister. She is (nin) years old. She's in the (therd) grade. I also have two brothers. My older brother is (tene). My other brother is just a baby.

eight	nine	ten
second	third	

129

Spectrum Spelling
Grade 2

Answer Key

Write the spelling word that fits each meaning.

1. A brown __deer__ ran into the woods.
2. I like soup with vegetables and __meat__.
3. My dog is digging a __hole__ in the dirt.
4. I will __meet__ my sister after school.
5. We __rode__ our bikes home.
6. My brother and I ate a __whole__ pizza.
7. There are many cars on the __road__ today.
8. The boys took off __their__ coats.
9. __There__ is a pear tree in my yard.
10. My dad's mom is my __grandmother__.

Write the spelling word or words that belong with each word.

1. parents — __mother__ __father__
2. grandparents — __grandfather__ __grandmother__
3. sister — __brother__
4. aunt — __uncle__

130

Write the spelling word that tells how many.

1. __five__
2. __two__
3. __eight__
4. __ten__
5. __seven__
6. __one__
7. __three__
8. __nine__
9. __four__
10. __six__

131

Say each word. Listen to the /ů/ sound. Write each word.

Spelling Tip	The /ů/ sound is often spelled **oo** or **u**.

Spelling Words

look	__look__
put	__put__
cook	__cook__
wood	__wood__
took	__took__
full	__full__
hook	__hook__
good	__good__
book	__book__
stood	__stood__

132

Words in Context
Write the missing spelling words.

My mom likes to
__cook__.
She makes (cookies) and meats.
She doesn't __look__
in a __book__,
when she whips up her treats.
She has a small (nook)
that is __full__ of her <u>tools</u>.
And hung from a __hook__,
A list of kitchen rules:
"__Put__ all dishes away.
Sweep up the __wood__ <u>floors</u>.
If you've done all the chores,
I will have a __good__ day."
I once __took__ a turn.
I __stood__ in her place.
But the <u>food</u> started to burn.
There was smoke everyplace.

Challenge
Circle the other words in the rhyme with the /ů/ sound.
Underline the words with **oo** that do not have the /ů/ sound.

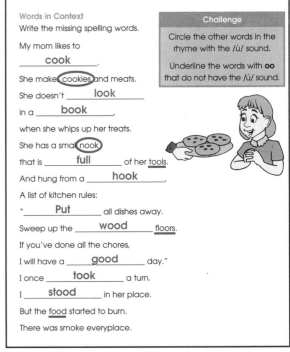

133

Answer Key

Answer Key

Fun with Words

Write the spelling word that completes each tongue-twister.

1. Cara can _____cook_____ corn on the cob.
2. Pat ___put___ a plum on Paul's plate.
3. Tara _____took_____ ten turns trying to tell time.
4. Stan stopped and _____stood_____ still.
5. _____Look_____ at Len's little lamb.
6. Hank hung his hat on a _____hook_____.

Words Across the Curriculum

Say each science word. Then, write each word.

1. push ____push____   3. wool ____wool____
2. pull ____pull____   4. brook ____brook____

Write the spelling word or words that complete each sentence.

1. A ____brook____ is a creek, or small stream.
2. ____Wool____ is made from sheep's hair.
3. A force can be a ____push____ or a ____pull____.

134

Words in Writing

Write a list that tells what chores you do at home. Use at least three of the words from the box.

| look | cook | took | hook | book | push | wool |
| put | wood | full | good | stood | pull | brook |

_____

_____

_____   Answers will vary.

_____

_____

Dictionary Practice

Some words have more than one meaning. A dictionary tells when a word is a noun, a verb, or both. Write the five spelling words and science words that can be a noun and a verb.

I took one **step**.
I will **step** over the puddle.

1. ____cook____   3. ____look____   5. ____push____
2. ____hook____   4. ____pull____

135

Say each word. Listen for the /ou/ sound. Write each word.

| Spelling Tip | The /ou/ sound can be spelled **ou** or **ow**. |

Spelling Words

out — ____out____

owl — ____owl____

now — ____now____

loud — ____loud____

count — ____count____

down — ____down____

sound — ____sound____

south — ____south____

ground — ____ground____

around — ____around____

136

Words in Context

Write the missing spelling words.

Gone for the Winter

_____Now_____ that it is almost winter, many birds will fly ____south____. If you look ____out____ your window, you might see some of them. So many birds fly together that you can't ____count____ them. This helps to protect them from bigger birds, such as an eagle or an ____owl____. These big birds can swoop ____down____ on smaller birds without making a ____sound____. The birds fly for many hours before they land on the ____ground____ to rest. After they rest, some birds make ____loud____ sounds. The other birds gather ____around____ them. All the birds fly off together again.

Challenge

Circle the other words in the report with /ou/ sound.

Underline the words with **ou** or **ow** that don't have the /ou/ sound.

137

Answer Key

Spectrum Spelling
Grade 2

Page 138

Fun with Words

Use the clues to complete the puzzle with spelling words.

Down

1. opposite of north
3. opposite of up
5. bird with big eyes
7. opposite of in

Across

2. noise
4. at this time
6. opposite of quiet
8. find out how many

Crossword solution:
- 1 (down): s o u t h
- 2 (across): s o u n d
- 3 (down): d o w n
- 5 (down): o w l
- 4 (across): n o w
- 6 (across): l o u d
- 7 (down): u
- 8 (across): c o u n t

Words Across the Curriculum

Say each social studies word. Then, write each word.

1. town — **town**
2. crowd — **crowd**
3. found — **found**
4. crown — **crown**

Write the social studies word that completes each sentence.

1. A king sometimes wears a **crown** .
2. A **town** is smaller than a city.
3. A **crowd** of people was there to hear the band.
4. A girl on my street **found** my lost dog.

138

Page 139

Words in Writing

Write a short report about an animal. Use at least three of the words from the box.

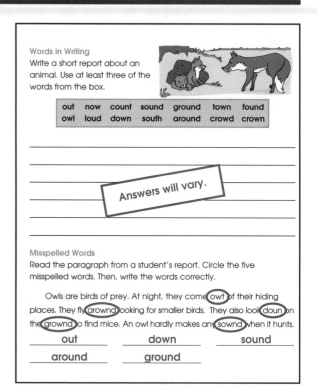

| out | now | count | sound | ground | town | found |
| owl | loud | down | south | around | crowd | crown |

Answers will vary.

Misspelled Words

Read the paragraph from a student's report. Circle the five misspelled words. Then, write the words correctly.

Owls are birds of prey. At night, they come (owt) of their hiding places. They fly (arownd) looking for smaller birds. They also look (down) on the (grownd) to find mice. An owl hardly makes any (sownd) when it hunts.

out   **down**   **sound**
around   **ground**

139

Page 140

Say each word. Look at the spelling. Write each word.

| **Spelling Tip** | A contraction is made of two words with one or more letters left out. An apostrophe is a mark that shows where some letters have been left out. |

Spelling Words

I'm	**I'm**
can't	**can't**
you'll	**you'll**
I'll	**I'll**
it's	**it's**
there's	**there's**
we'll	**we'll**
don't	**don't**
that's	**that's**
wouldn't	**wouldn't**

140

Page 141

Words in Context

Write the contractions that replace the underlined words.

| **Challenge** |
| Circle the other contractions in the letter. |

Birthday Party

Dear Josh,

Thank you for inviting me to your party! (I am) **I'm** really glad that you asked me. I know (it is) **it's** going to be a lot of fun. I (do not) **don't** know if my sister can come. (She'd) really like to, but (she's) got soccer practice that day. She (can not) **can't** miss it or she (would not) **wouldn't** get to play in the next game. If (there is) **there's** any way she can go to your party, (we will) **we'll** go together. (I've) already gotten your birthday present. (You will) **you'll** really like it. (That is) **that's** all (I will) **I'll** say about it until your party!

Your friend,
Mickey

141

Answer Key

Fun with Words
Follow the steps to make the spelling word contractions.

1. we will – wi + ' = __we'll__

2. do not – o + ' = __don't__

3. I will – wi + ' = __I'll__

4. I am – a + ' = __I'm__

5. can not – no + ' = __can't__

6. there is – i + ' = __there's__

7. you will – wi + ' = __you'll__

8. that is – s + ' = __that's__

Words Across the Curriculum (Language Arts icon)
Say each contraction. Then, write the contraction.

1. he's __he's__   3. she's __she's__

2. we're __we're__   4. they're __they're__

Write each contraction where it belongs.

My brother is ten years old. __He's__ older than I am.

My sister is only one. __She's__ a baby.

__They're__ both at the park now. When they get home,

__we're__ all going to have lunch.

142

Words in Writing
Write a letter to a friend. Use at least three
of the words from the box.

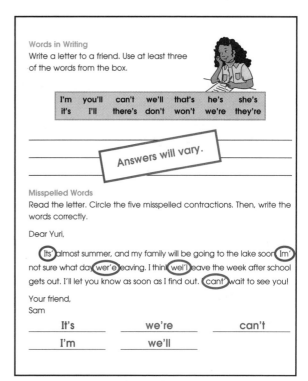

| I'm | you'll | can't | we'll | that's | he's | she's |
| it's | I'll | there's | don't | won't | we're | they're |

Answers will vary.

Misspelled Words
Read the letter. Circle the five misspelled contractions. Then, write the
words correctly.

Dear Yuri,

(Its') almost summer, and my family will be going to the lake soon. (Im')
not sure what day (wer'e) leaving. I think (wel'l) leave the week after school
gets out. I'll let you know as soon as I find out. (cant') wait to see you!

Your friend,
Sam

__It's__   __we're__   __can't__

__I'm__   __we'll__

143

Say each word. Listen to the two words that make up the word. Write
each word.

| Spelling Tip | A compound word is made up of two smaller words. |

Spelling Words

into   __into__

without   __without__

sometimes   __sometimes__

today   __today__

myself   __myself__

everyone   __everyone__

weekend   __weekend__

bedroom   __bedroom__

outside   __outside__

nothing   __nothing__

144

Words in Context
Write the missing spelling words.

Workday

| Challenge |
| Circle the other compound words in the story. |

__Today__ is Saturday. That means __everyone__

in my family has to do chores. I have to clean my

__bedroom__ all by __myself__. I have to make sure

that __nothing__ is out of place. Then, I have to wash my

clothes and put them __into__ my closet. I also have to

help my sister clean the (bathroom) (upstairs.) After we've done our

chores (inside) the house, we go __outside__ to work in the

yard. __Sometimes__, we rakes leaves. Other times, we pull the

weeds from the (flowerbeds.) When we've done __everything__

on our list of chores, we can enjoy the rest of the __weekend__.

Word Building
Combine the words to make compound words.

1. sail + boat = __sailboat__

2. birth + day = __birthday__

3. may + be = __maybe__

4. note + book = __notebook__

145

Spectrum Spelling
Grade 2

Answer Key

195

Answer Key

Answer Key

Fun with Words

Write the spelling word that includes one of the words from each compound word.

1. cookout ___outside___
2. daytime ___today___
3. himself ___myself___
4. nowhere ___nothing___
5. something ___sometimes___
6. bathroom ___bedroom___
7. within ___into___
8. bookend ___weekend___

Words Across the Curriculum

Say each social studies word. Then, write the word.

1. downtown ___downtown___
2. mailbag ___mailbag___
3. classroom ___classroom___
4. daylight ___daylight___

Write each social studies word next to its definition.

1. a place for students to learn ___classroom___
2. a sack to carry letters in ___mailbag___
3. the time when the sun shines ___daytime___
4. the middle of a city ___downtown___

146

Words in Writing

Write about something your family does on the on the weekends. Use at least three of the words from the box.

| into | sometimes | myself | weekend | outside | downtown | classroom |
| without | today | everyone | bedroom | nothing | mailbag | daylight |

Answers will vary.

Misspelled Words

Read the description. Circle the five misspelled words. Then, write the words correctly.

Every weekend in the summer, (everone) in my family comes to my house. My cousins and I play games in my (bedrom) for a while. (Somtimes) we have a cookout (outcide) in the backyard. The food is always so good that there's (nothig) left over. I'm sad when everybody has to leave.

___everyone___ ___Sometimes___ ___nothing___
___bedroom___ ___outside___

147

Write the contraction for each pair of words.

1. you will ___you'll___
2. do not ___don't___
3. I am ___I'm___
4. there is ___there's___
5. can not ___can't___
6. I will ___I'll___
7. we will ___we'll___
8. it is ___it's___
9. that is ___that's___
10. will not ___won't___

Write the spelling word that completes each sentence.

1. Please hang your coat on the ___hook___.
2. An ___owl___ sleeps during the day and hunts at night.
3. There is no school on the ___weekend___.
4. Some floors are made of ___wood___.
5. I can ___count___ to 100.
6. On a hot summer day, ___sometimes___ I go swimming.

148

Write the spelling word that means the opposite.

1. bad ___good___
2. in ___out___
3. north ___south___
4. something ___nothing___
5. gave ___took___
6. up ___down___
7. empty ___full___
8. inside ___outside___
9. sat ___stood___
10. quiet ___loud___
11. no one ___everyone___
12. later ___now___

149

Notes

Notes

Notes

Notes

Notes

Notes

Notes

Notes

Notes

Notes

Notes

Notes